RETURN OF THE WHITE CANONS

RETURN OF THE WHITE CANONS

The Modern Norbertines in Britain

Aidan Nichols

GRACEWING

First published in England in 2024
by
Gracewing
2 Southern Avenue
Leominster
Herefordshire HR6 0QF
United Kingdom
www.gracewing.co.uk

The right of Aidan Nichols to be identified
as the author of this work has been asserted in accordance
with the Copyright, Designs and Patents Act 1988.

ISBN 978 085244 833 5

Cover image:
Clothing Day in Storrington Priory (Muston Priory Archives)
Cover design by Bernardita Peña Hurtado

Typeset by Word and Page, Chester, UK

CONTENTS

PREFACE

'As one of the great religious orders, the white canons of Prémontré have a place in European history.' With these words H. M. Colvin, Fellow of St John's College, Oxford, opened the study of *The White Canons in England*, which he published in 1951 by courtesy of the Clarendon Press. As Colvin pointed out, they have their historians—but not (he might have added) for his native land's nineteenth and twentieth centuries when attempts to re-implant them in Britain (which here means overwhelmingly England) sought to renew some of the patterns—and even, in one instance, locations—of their pre-Reformation existence in this island.

I am grateful for help received from Fr Thomas Swaffer, O.Praem., and Fr Martin Gosling, O.Praem., Administrator and Provisor, respectively, of St Mary's Priory, Muston, and from Fr Gildas Parry, O.Praem., Librarian of Our Lady of Sorrows Priory, Peckham, London SE15, as also from Fr Michael Gallagher, O.Praem., now resident at St Joseph's Home, Longsight, Manchester, for information about the last years and closure of Corpus Christi Priory, Miles Platting. I am also indebted to Pater Kees van Heijst, O.Praem., Archivist of the Abbey of Onze-Lieve-Vrouw at Tongerlo, to Fra François-Marie Pourcelet, Chevalier de Justice in the Order of St John of Jerusalem, Archivist of the Abbaye Saint-Michel de Frigolet, to Mr Paul Carr, the Archivist of the diocese of Salford, to the Revd Anthony Dolan and the Revd Kevin Athaide, respectively the emeritus and present archivists of the diocese of Nottingham, to Ms Lynsey Nairn, the Archivist of the Marquesses of Bute at Mountstuart, to the Revd John Butters, outgoing editor of the *Northern Catholic Calendar*, to the Revd Bernard Partington, sometime parish priest of Mater Amabilis church, Ambleside, to Mr Michael Roberts of Spalding, to Mr Philip Orpwood of Storrington, and to Father Saba Al Andary and Mrs Samar Al Andary, and the Revd Charles Hadley and Mrs Felicity Hadley, of the ecumenical organization Chemin Neuf, for aid in my visit to Our Lady of England Priory at Storrington; the Fathers and Brothers of the Manchester Oratory for their generous hospitality during my enquiries into the history of Corpus Christi Priory, Miles Platting, and, last but not least to Dom Geoffrey Scott, Librarian and Archivist of Douai Abbey.

This modest essay is the only recompense I can offer for kindnesses by English Norbertines in my own recent wanderings between worlds.

It is not the last word on its chosen subject, but it is, I believe, by far the fullest account available hitherto.

The book introduces the reader to its subject by a brief overview of the Order's twelfth century origins and its history up to and including the modern period. Attempts at re-implantation are then described in the context of the two European abbeys (Tongerlo and Frigolet) responsible for the new seedlings in the Protestant island. In the context of the Catholic Revival, Recusant gentry and aristocracy, Tractarian converts, and an empress in exile were only too eager to promote their own spiritual projects by profiting from both the numerous vocations to Religious life in post-Revolutionary Belgium and the expulsion of the 'Unregistered Congregations' by an anti-clerical regime in France. Though the results sometimes verged on the tragi-comic, much excellent pastoral work was done, especially by the more successful foundations, one of which found itself caught up in the literary and theological history of England.

The book ends by considering the present and future possibilities open to the present-day successors of the historic figures here portrayed.

St Birinus' Rectory, Dorchester-on-Thames, Oxfordshire

Feast of St John Henry Newman, 2023

Introducing the Premonstratensians

T HE PREMONSTRATENSIAN ORDER, founded by St Norbert of Xanten
(c. 1075/1080–1134), was one of the principal monastic institutions
in mediaeval England (and the source of foundations in Scotland,
Ireland, and Wales), with some thirty-six houses to its credit.[1] None of
them were especially large and their outreach was limited to the pastoral
care of the parishes in which they ministered. In continental Europe the
Order's influence was a good deal wider, whether, in the Middle Ages,
through missionary work to the east of the Germanic lands, or, in the
Europe of the Catholic Reformation, by routes cultural and scholarly.

In their different ways the abbeys reflected in some manner the pre-
occupations of St Norbert himself: an itinerant evangelist who saw monasteries as contemplative resources for preaching and pastoral care.[2] In
that sense, the Premonstratensian Order constitutes a kind of historical
presupposition for the much more celebrated Order of Preachers whose
founder, Dominic of Caleruega (1170–1221), was formed in this kind of
'canon regular' vocation—irrespective of whether he had once belonged,
as has been proposed, to a Norbertine abbey. The Dominicans might
be called Premonstratensians rendered more apostolically effective by
their distinctive organization as well as more theologically alert by their
early production of a thinker of stellar magnitude, Thomas Aquinas
(1225–74). But they lost out on 'abbey life'.[3]

1 The standard work is H. M. Colvin, *The White Canons in England* (Oxford:
Clarendon Press, 1951), though since the writing of that book much has been
done on the history (and archaeological remains) of individual abbeys/priories.
An outstanding study, based on the richest extant manuscript source, is Joseph
A. Gribbin, *The Premonstratensian Order in Late Mediaeval England* (Woodbridge:
Boydell & Brewer, 2012).

2 Dominique-Marie Dauzet, *Petite vie de saint Norbert* (Paris: Desclée de Brouwer, 2013).

3 For a fuller, if more personal, Dominican-tinged view of St Norbert and his
Order see Aidan Nichols, *Apologia—A Memoir* (Leominster: Gracewing, 2023), pp.
123–7.

Wiped out by the sixteenth-century Reformation in Scandinavia, the British Isles, and Northern Germany, the Premonstratensians were decimated elsewhere by the combined effect of the French Revolution and Napoleonic and post-Napoleonic policies of secularization. Yet in some places the abbeys had retained (Austria-Hungary) or quickly recovered (the Low Countries), a lively existence. In the later nineteenth and early twentieth centuries that made possible a significant contribution to the missionary expansion of the Church in the Americas (United States, Canada, Brazil, Chile), India, and Africa (Congo).[4]

The course taken by their re-implanting in England (with a toe-hold or two in Scotland) was chequered. For the believing historian its outcome, while not nugatory (at least in England), is nonetheless disappointing. Quite apart from some poor internal decisions of the Order's membership, the contemporary background—the demographic decline of the English Catholic Church of the 'Second Spring' (in parallel with trends elsewhere in the West, including north of the Anglo-Scottish Border)—is necessarily pertinent, though not a topic that can be handled here.[5] In any case, the Church historian, in his capacity as a 'professional rememberer', should not fail to note the apostolic, educational, and pastoral effort of the canons in missions and parishes,[6] or the energies invested by priests and brothers in attempts to build a conventual life suited to regular clergy whose vocation was set in a monastic mould. 'Re-implantation', however limited its longer-term success, involved all of this inherently valuable work.

---

4 The chief recent histories are Bernard Ardura, *Prémontrés. Histoire et spiritualité* (Saint-Étienne: Université de Saint-Étienne, 1995); Dominique-Marie Dauzet, *L'Ordre de Prémontré. Neuf cents ans d'histoire* (Paris: Salvator, 2021).

5 For the vagaries of the post-Reformation period, see Edward Norman, *The English Catholic Church in the Nineteenth Century* (Oxford: Clarendon Press, 1984); Edward Norman, *Roman Catholicism in England from the Elizabethan Settlement to the Second Vatican Council* (New York: Oxford University Press, 1985); Stephen Bullivant, *Mass Exodus: Catholic Disaffiliation in Britain and America since Vatican II* (Oxford: Oxford University Press, 2019, 2nd edition).

6 Strictly speaking, 'parishes' in the full canonical sense were not erected in England until 1918.

Flemish Beginnings:
The Tongerlo Background

THE BELGIAN ABBEY OF TONGERLO was founded in 1130 from St Michael's in Antwerp, one of Norbert's own immediate foundations (or re-foundations, since it had been a house of unreformed canons in time past).[1] Its abbots were major figures in the duchy of Brabant where the later dukes were those of Burgundy and, after 1482, Spanish Habsburgs. At the Peace of Utrecht in 1715 the Spanish Netherlands became Austrian, a problematic outcome for Tongerlo, as for other Flemish abbeys, once the emperors adopted, later that century, an Enlightenment ideology for which conventual life, purely as such, was neither philosophically intelligible nor socially useful.

In the course of its long history the abbey developed a fine book-collection, and after the suppression of the Jesuit Society enriched it with the historical library of the Bollandists,[2] whose work in erudite pursuit of critical lives of the saints the Premonstratensians inherited. But that was until the French Revolution when in 1796 the church and most of the conventual buildings were razed by the Revolutionary armies. Tongerlo had numbered some 150 brethren before the storm broke.[3] As everywhere in revolutionary France and its conquered territories Religious life was forbidden. But the canons regular could be cunning. So far as they could they sought to hide their treasures,

1 Waltman van Spilbeeck, *De abdij van Tongerloo. Geschiedkundige navorsingen* (Lier and Geel: Taymans-Nezy, 1888, reprinted in facsimile Averbode: Abdij Averbode, 1997). A condensed history is found in L. C. Van Dyck, *The Norbertine Abbey of Tongerlo* (Westerlo-Tongerlo: Norbertijnenabdij & Stichting Monumenten en Landscapszorg, nd).

2 Hugues Lamy, 'L'Œuvre des Bollandistes à l'abbaye de Tongerlo', *Analecta Praemonstratensia* 2 (1926), pp. 294–306, 379–89; 3 (1927), pp. 61–79, 156–78, 284–313.

3 Bernard Ardura, *Premostratensi. Novi secoli di storia e spiritualità di un grande Ordine Religioso* (Bologna: Edizioni Studio Domenicano, 1997), p. 337. Italian translation (with a new introduction) of the work cited in note 3 above.

whether books or ornaments, and wherever possible even to save part of their buildings.[4]

Once the Revolutionary (and Napoleonic) wave had spent itself, appeals for restoration to the Congress of Vienna were possible but fruitless. The post-Congress Kingdom of the Netherlands was hardly more encouraging. But in 1835, after Belgium had been granted independence under the terms of the 1830 Treaty of London, it was feasible for the surviving canons to resume recruiting, though the new government was Liberal, and would recognize neither the legal personality of the abbeys nor their right to nominate the pastors of 'incorporated' parishes. In 1838 the community was officially restored, if not on its proper site, and in 1840 the remaining canons bought back what was left of the ancient Tongerlo. A new church and monastery were built between 1852 and 1858.[5] Extensions, improvements, and repairs, continued until after the First World War, though a disastrous fire in 1929 meant that much would have to be done all over again.

Missionary work outside the old Christendom began under Abbot Thomas Louis Heylen (1856–1941), later bishop of Namur.[6] Heylen had entered Religious life with a view to work in England, and received the name in religion of St Thomas of Canterbury (otherwise Thomas Becket, *c.* 1120–70). As abbot he found more demanding mission territory in the 'Congo Free State' (rather a misnomer, except that it was free from the constitutional arrangements of Belgium, so as to be the more firmly under the personal direction of the king of the Belgians).[7] Heylen was evidently a man of parts. He sought ways to apply the 'Catholic social teaching' so recently refreshed by Pope Leo XIII (1810–1903). At a crucial stage in its existence he directed the movement of 'International Eucharistic Congresses' which began in 1881. He played an important role in the integration into the Order of the abbey of Frigolet and its dependent houses, the 'Primitive Observance Congregation of France' (on which more anon). And he also oversaw the production of the 1896 *Breviarium praemonstratense*, which helped give back to the Order something of its mediaeval liturgical inheritance.

---

4 *Ibid.*, p. 334.
5 *Ibid.*, p. 335.
6 For this figure, see Donatien de Clercq, O.Praem., 'Monseigneur Thomas Louis Heylen', in Dominique-Marie Dauzet, Martine Plouvier and Cécile Souchon (ed.), *Les Prémontrés au XIXe siècle: traditions et renouveau* (Paris: Cerf, 2000), pp. 261–9. On his episcopal labours, see J. E. Jansen, *Monseigneur Thomas-Louis Heylen, évêque de Namur. Son action sociale et religieuse pendant vingt-cinq ans d'épiscopat* (Namur: Wesmael-Charlier, 1924).
7 Richard Dane Lokando, *Prémontrés et dominicains belges au Congo: Uele 1898–1924* (Paris: L'Harmattan, 2018).

The abbey of Our Dear Lady (Onze-Lieve-Vrouw) of Tongerlo was extremely flourishing until the post-Conciliar period. In 1924 Tongerlo founded the dependent priory which in 1964 became the abbey of Kilnacrott, Ballyjamesduff, County Cavan, later decimated—indeed, destroyed—by one of the worst child-abuse scandals in contemporary Church history. In 1929 Tongerlo refounded (for the second time since the Revolution) the Walloon abbey of Leffe, in Dinant.[8] In 1948 its conventus peaked at the extraordinarily high number of 234 Religious. In 1949 it opened a priory in Quebec, which moved site within that Canadian Province in 1968. In 1966 former Tongerlo missionaries in the Congo, which by that date was independent under the name 'Zaire'(now the Democratic Republic of the Congo), went to Chile and founded a new priory at Chiguyante, Gran Concepción, with a parish in the capital, Santiago. At the time of writing (2023), one canon remains there, the abbey's last missionary.[9] Tongerlo also produced the celebrated 'bacon priest' Werenfried van Straaten (1913–2003), who did so much for the often displaced and ill-fed population of post-War Germany and subsequently founded for the benefit of the pastoral life of the Church behind the Iron Curtain the highly active Catholic charity Aid to the Church in Need, the work of which is now global in extent.[10] Tongerlo was, then, an historic community with a great track record, well capable of making a foundation (or more) in England.

It might not be entirely irrelevant to recall that Flanders and England had connexions over and above the mediaeval wool trade, which made the fortunes of East Anglia as its seaports traded with those of the Low Countries. England and Flanders had once shared their rulers—in the reign of Mary Tudor (1516–58), and her consort Philip of Spain (1527–98). The Spanish—later the Austrian—Netherlands, under their Habsburg sovereigns, had given shelter to several of the communities of English Catholic Religious (monks, friars, nuns) who found refuge from persecution, or harassment, overseas—the English Dominicans (and Dominicanesses) among them.[11] These historic links created a certain affinity.

---

8 'Second time': the Belgian exile of canons from the Provençal abbey of Frigolet, from 1903 to (towards) 1922, was largely spent in this recovered former abbey, from which the priests made preaching-sorties into France dressed (for the sake of accommodation to the civil law) in the black soutanes of the secular clergy, Bernard Ardura, *L'Abbaye Saint-Michel de Frigolet, 1858–2008. Un siècle et demi d'histoire des Prémontrés en Provence* (Paris, Les-Plans-sur-Bex: Parole et Silence, 2008), p. 95.

9 Information provided by Kees van Heijst, O.Praem., in a conversation of 12 September 2023.

10 Jean Bourdarias, *Père Werenfried, un géant de la charité* (Paris: Fayard, 1996).

11 Peter Guilday, *The English Catholic Refugees on the Continent, I. The English Colleges and Convents in the Catholic Low Countries, 1558–1795* (London: Longmans, 1914).

─ 3 ─

Wheatfields and Tulips: Tongerlo in the East of England

I N THE LATER NINETEENTH AND EARLY TWENTIETH CENTURIES Tongerlo would establish a cluster of parishes in Lincolnshire (North and South Holland) and South Yorkshire, the latter area bordering as it did on North Holland.

The enterprise began in 1872 with Crowle, an agricultural market town in North Lincolnshire, on the Isle of Axholme, a district where, until the efforts of a Dutch engineer commissioned by Charles I (1600–49), towns and villages were raised on mounds surrounded by marsh.[1] The key figure in the Crowle implantation was Thomas Arthur Young (1805–91) of Kingerby Hall, Market Rasen, with a subsidiary but vital intermediary role played by John Philips, a London bookseller who ran an additional business office in Antwerp.[2] Philips was personally acquainted with the principal mover and shaker in the re-founding of Tongerlo, Peter Hubert Evermode Backx (1805–68).[3] Young offered Tongerlo a church and a house, with land, for a canonry. But why?

He had come across a tiny, printed engraving of a woodcut showing St Norbert as apostle of the Holy Eucharist—a reference to his role in the suppression of the anti-sacramentarian heresy of Tanchelm (c. 1070–1115)—and was intrigued to discover the existence of pre-Reformation Premonstratensian sites in Lincolnshire. Actually, there were nine of them, more than for any other English county. In a letter to a local nobleman, seeking to commend his project, he explained: 'I am a

---

1 J. Korthals-Alles, *Sir Cornelius Vermuyden: The Lifework of a Great Anglo-Dutch-man in Land Reclamation and Drainage* (London: Williams and Norgate, 1925).

2 *St Norbert's Parish, Crowle. Centenary Booklet, 1872–1972* (Storrington: Norbertine Press, 1972). Muston Archives.

3 L. C. van Dijck, 'Evermodus P. H. Backx, de tweede stichter van de abdij van Tongerlo. Bidrage tot een levenscheets, 1835–1845', *De Lindeboom* [Tilburg] 5 (1981), pp. 158–204.

resident in an extinct Premonstratensian parish—it had formerly been appropriated to Drax Priory in Yorkshire'.[4] The print in question was copied under the heading 'The Engraving that Occasioned our Return to England' by an evidently pious (in the Virgilian sense) English Premonstratensian, Patrick Kerigan (1895–1977), and attached to a piece of notepaper headed 'The Priory, Crowle, Near Scunthorpe', now held in the Muston Archives.[5] For a Catholic of means in nineteenth-century England, such a discovery was a sufficient incentive to be a Religious founder. Convents and monasteries were mushrooming, among High Church Anglicans as well as Roman Catholics, despite—or because of—spirited Victorian disapproval.[6]

A suitable location soon suggested itself. A Crowle inhabitant, an Anglicized Italian, James Walker (aka Girolamo Vaccari), appealed to Young for help in establishing a place for Catholic worship. Letters from Young on the topic begin as early as the spring of 1862, when he wrote to Walker's Sussex-born wife, née Hannah Rogers,[7] 'The spiritual destitution of the Catholics at Crowle and its neighbourhood is extremely pitiable as you represent them'.[8] Gas production, chiefly for street lighting, was attracting an influx of Irish workers; Walker was their sympathetic foreman. Though the east of England lay furthest from the ports of entry of the Irish, the sheer size of the predominantly Catholic immigration from 'John Bull's other island' was inevitably a factor in the case for Tongerlo's Lincolnshire foundations.[9] Walker's entreaties did not persuade Richard Butler Roskell (1817–83), the second bishop of Nottingham. A scattered and far from wealthy Catholic population did not have the resources to build a church or the numbers to justify

4 Letter of 16 July 1872 from Thomas Arthur Young to Lord Herries, Tongerlo Archives, E2 Engeland en Storrington, Box 1, 2/1.

5 Kerigan, a Mancunian, clothed at Tongerlo in 1919, had been made parish priest of Crowle in 1940. Thus the Muston Necrology. A booklet published for his twenty-fifth anniversary as parish priest of Crowle (*Silver Jubilee of Rev. A. P. Kerigan, C. R. P., 1940–1965*, in the Muston Archives) adds the information that from 1924 to 1939 he functioned as a founding member of Tongerlo's newly created Kilnacrott Priory where, in his capacity as its first bursar, he was largely responsible for the development of its juniorate, 'St Norbert's College', (much) later to become so unfortunately notorious for deficiencies in 'safeguarding'.

6 A. M. Allchin, *The Silent Rebellion. Anglican Religious Communities, 1845–1900* (London: SCM Press, 1958); René Kollar, 'Religious Orders', in Sally Mitchell (ed.), *Victorian Britain. An Encyclopedia* (New York, and London: Garland, 1988), pp. 666–7.

7 Alan Gidney, *The Parish and Church of St Norbert's, Crowle. 125 Years of Catholicism in Crowle* (Crowle: no publisher, 1999), p. 2.

8 Letter of 27 March 1862 from Thomas Young to Mrs Walker. Muston Archives.

9 Donald M. MacRaild, *Irish Migrants in Modern Britain, 1750–1922* (Basingstoke: Macmillan, 1999).

the more than occasional services of a pastor.[10] Young could provide the cash outlay but not conjure up a priest. So Philips put Young in touch with Abbot Jean Chrysostome de Swert of Tongerlo (1834–87),[11] with productive results. Young was fortunate in finding in office in the Belgian monastery this 'lettered and cultivated abbot'.[12] Meanwhile, the bishop was only too glad to be rid of a burden, writing early in 1871 to describe his 'delight' at the notion of Belgian priests willing to serve in the Isle of Axholme.[13] His delight faded somewhat on discovering Young's plan was for the properties he provided—in the plural, since soon enough Young would extend his gaze from north Lincolnshire to south—were to remain in perpetuity in possession of the Flemish abbey. As Bishop Roskell would tell Abbot de Swert (to no avail), permitting the foundation of a 'Religious mission' would be a 'matter for rather serious consideration, as it is of course an impediment to the establishment of a secular mission, and therefore to a certain extent transfers the management of the locality from the Diocese to the Religious Order'.[14] But this was exactly what Young had intended all along.

Some enlightenment as to Young's background is offered by the *Records of the English Province of the Society of Jesus* in an article, subsequently re-printed, consisting of notes provided to the editor, the principal topic of which was 'Thomas Arthur Young' of 'Kingerby Manor'. Young was the scion of a Recusant family of Welsh origin though the elder branch were Protestants, created baronets by Charles I in 1629. The cadet line was devout: Young's sister Juliana was a Visitandine nun at Westbury-on-Trym. And the Youngs were wealthy. His grandfather Isaac Young had bought Kingerby in 1785 (previously the Hall was leased

---

10 Until the 1873 *Catholic Directory* for Great Britain, Crowle (along with Epworth) appears as served from Gainsborough where a church dedicated to St Thomas of Canterbury had been erected in 1866: *The Catholic Directory, Ecclesiastical Register and Almanac for the Year of Our Lord 1872* (London: Burns, Oates, & Co., 1872), p. 186. I am grateful to Dom Geoffrey Scott of Douai Abbey for giving me access to the monastic Library's run of these 'Directories' on a visit of 29 June 2023.

11 For this figure, see Ronny de Cuyper, *Joannes Chrysostomus de Swert, vijftigste abt van Tongerlo, 1867/8–1887* (Leuven: Katholieke Universiteit, 1981).

12 Dominique-Marie Dauzet, 'Jean Chrysostome de Swert, abbé de Tongerlo (1834–87) à travers sa correspondance', in Dominique-Marie Dauzet and Martine Plouvier (ed.), *Abbatiat et abbés dans l'Ordre de Prémontré* (Turnhout: Brepols, 2015), pp. 377–90, and here at p. 386. Unfortunately, the latter study confines itself almost exclusively to the correspondence of Abbot de Swert with the prioress of the Norbertine nuns of Bonlieu, Marie Odiot de la Paillonne (1840–1905).

13 Letter of 15 February 1871 from Bishop Roskell of Nottingham to Thomas Arthur Young. Tongerlo Archives, E2 Engeland en Storrington, Box 1, 1.

14 Letter of 9 October 1875 from Bishop Roskell of Nottingham to Abbot de Swert, Tongerlo Archives, E2 Engeland en Storrington, Box 1, 2/2.

from its owners) 'as soon as the Act of Parliament gave permission to Catholics to purchase land'.[15] Thomas Young was conscious of the dual responsibilities he had inherited: those of a landowning gentleman who was also an 'Old' Catholic. He had once furnished the indefatigable Jesuit historian Br Henry Foley (1811–91), with some material on the connexions of the Lincolnshire Youngs with the Society of Jesus.[16] The turn from the Jesuits to the Premonstratensians reflects the 'Gothick' or mediaevalist traits of the nineteenth-century Catholic revival, a feature of its age.[17]

A rare vignette of Young entered the Muston Archives by a circuitous route. The English Jesuit Clement Tigar (1892–1976), a tireless educator of priests but best known for his work in promoting the 'causes' of the martyrs of England and Wales, edited a popular magazine called *Stella Maris* (its circulation at one point topped 100,000). In this capacity, he published in June 1959 an article on the White Canons. This elicited a letter to the editor from a correspondent, J. J. Dwyer, a man in his eightieth year with local Lincolnshire knowledge. His uncle, Canon James Dwyer, so the younger Dwyer explained, had been missionary rector of Market Rasen at the time when Young had withdrawn from Kingerby manor to a 'smallish' residence half a mile from that town. 'He was very much of the old school, dressed in black broadcloth, like Sir Robert Peel or the Duke of Wellington, and wore a kind of stock. In appearance and features he was something like J. H. Newman, but not tall, and he looked like a priest of Lingard's time. As long as he was able to go to church he sat alone in the front bench, left aisle. Later, my uncle used to take him Holy Communion, a service which he always rewarded with three sovereigns, "one for the Father, one for the Son, and one for the Holy Ghost". I have heard him say how he brought the C. R. P.'s [Canons Regular of Prémontré] back into England.'[18] And indeed,

15 Anonymous, 'The Young Family', re-printed from *Records of the English Province of the Society of Jesus* (np, nd), p. 10. Muston Archives. The Act of Parliament allowing Catholics to own land—the 'Papists' Act', better known by its more polite title, the 'First Catholic Relief Act'—is usually dated to 1788.

16 *Records of the English Province of the Society of Jesus. Historic Facts Illustrative of the Labours and Sufferings of its Members in the Sixteenth and Seventeenth Centuries*, vol. II = 'Second, Third, and Fourth Series' (London: Manresa Press, 1875), pp. 651–2.

17 Joanna Parker and Corinna Wagner (ed.), *The Oxford Handbook of Victorian Medievalism* (Oxford; Oxford University Press, 2020).

18 Letter of 29 May 1959 from J. J. Dwyer to Clement Tigar, SJ, forwarded by the latter to Prior Mathee of Storrington on 4 June 1959. Muston Archives. Sir Robert Peel (1788–1850) and Arthur Wellesley, first Duke of Wellington (1769–1852) were Tory prime ministers in the period 1828–52. John Henry Newman (1801–90) is too well known to require an explanatory note; 'Lingard' is the fine priest-historian John

Young could write to the Walters, husband and wife, in August 1871, 'the Bishop having given over the Isle of Axholme to the spiritual care of the Premonstratensian Fathers, and the Lord Abbot having accepted the offer and terms, I am now building not for the Bishop but for the Lord Abbot and the White Canons of St Norbert'.[19]

The Young/de Swert encounter led to the arrival at Crowle of Martin Geudens (1841–1913), previously novice master and theology professor at Tongerlo, and, as events proved, an enterprising and energetic figure. Born at Lichtaart, a village in the province of Antwerp, he had entered Tongerlo at the age of 19, and was ordained to the Catholic priesthood by Xavier de Mérode (1820–74), the controversial Belgian founder of the Papal Zouaves, *cameriere segreto* and later almoner in the household of Pius IX (1792–1878) the declaration of whose infallibility he opposed.[20] The Mérodes were the principal — not to say hegemonic — land-owning nobility in the region of the Province of Antwerp where Tongerlo was situated.[21] Young had been in personal contact with Geudens since, at any rate, 1872. Writing in July of that year, he apologized for the length of time taken, 'owing to my economy', to acquire land and build a pres-bytery and chapel, and, for future financial purposes, recommended Geudens to the possible patronage of other Catholics landowners in the Nottingham diocese, notably Lords Herries and Howard, and two commoners, Edward Chaloner and Richard Dawson.[22] Arrangements were made for a notary to meet the Tongerlo canons when they arrived

Lingard (1771–1851), the last forty years of whose life were spent as mission-rector of Hornby in the Lune Valley. See Peter Phillips, *John Lingard, Priest and Historian* (Leominster: Gracewing, 2008).

19 Letter of 24 August 1871 from Thomas Arthur Young to Mr and Mrs Walker. Muston Archives. Young certainly micromanaged the resultant project as frequent detailed letters over the next five years, directed to the first Superior of Crowle, and retained in the Muston Archives, make plain.

20 J. F. Sollier, 'Frédéric-François-Xavier Ghislain de Mérode', in *Catholic Ency-clopaedia* (New York: Robert Appleton, 1907–12), vol. X, *s.v.*

21 Still closely connected to the abbey of Tongerlo, the family have given their name to an area of south Brabant with many Norbertine associations: see the char-acteristically Flemish cyclist-oriented presentation of the region in Kris Rockelé and Marjan Cauwenberg (ed.), *Ontdek de Norbertijnen in de Merode* (Westerlo: de Merode Landschapspark, 2021). As late as 1933 a canon regular in the incorporated parish of St Joseph's, Moorends, would write to an abbot of Tongerlo wondering whether the Mérodes might be willing to subsidise the building of a worthier church, letter of 11 January 1933 from Jacob Slock, O.Praem., to Abbot Lamy. Tongerlo Archives, E2 Engeland en Storrington, Box 5, 27.

22 Letter of 15 July 1872 from Thomas Arthur Young to Martin Geudens, O.Praem. Tongerlo Archives, E2 England en Storrington, Box 1, 1.

by steamship from Antwerp at Kingston-upon-Hull,[23] and to take part in the forthcoming celebrations for the anniversary of Bishop Roskell's consecration at Nottingham. Good episcopal relations, after all, were a necessity. More practically, Young proposed that Geudens should also travel to Gainsborough to meet the secular clergyman who hitherto had responsibility for the 'poor Axholmites', and in that way obtain potentially useful information about local conditions.[24]

In 1874, with the aid of his confrere Basil Dockx (1846–1920), hitherto the 'provisor' (bursar) of the abbey of Tongerlo, Geudens opened a church in the Early English style dedicated to the holy patriarch, St Norbert. It remains the only church in Britain with this exclusive patronage.[25] For the benefit of the parish, a Catholic school was started nearby in the following year.[26] A subject, after Abbot de Swert's death in 1887, of Abbot Heylen, it was unsurprising that Geudens made a special effort to encourage Eucharistic devotion. Until the Second Vatican Council (1962–5) Corpus Christi processions at the Crowle priory attracted coachloads of the faithful from the major towns of the locality, notably Doncaster and Scunthorpe. But from the years of his Tongerlo teaching career he retained a scholarly mien despite the ministerial burdens he carried in England. A set of letters to Geudens from the English Catholic antiquarian and liturgical scholar Edmund Bishop (1846–1917), chiefly on the mediaeval evidence for Premonstratensians in England, bears its own witness.[27] It might also be noted that Geudens was known to Newman, who in 1886 wrote thanking him for the gift of a metrical version of the life of St Norbert published by Abbot de Swert that same year.[28]

23 Letter of 12 August 1872 from Thomas Arthur Young to Martin Geudens, O.Praem. Tongerlo Archives, E2 England en Storrington, Box 1, 1.

24 Letter of 8 September 1872 from Thomas Arthur Young to Martin Geudens, O.Praem. Tongerlo Archives, E2 England en Storrington, Box 1, 1.

25 'Exclusive' in the sense of excluding reference to the Blessed Virgin Mary and any other saint. The title did, however, include the words 'and the Blessed Sacrament'. Geudens explained this duality in the course of a printed Public Appeal for funds. Since Norbert was a 'zealous defender of this great Mystery', quite appropriately his new 'church and residence' (at Crowle) were 'built to be a lasting memorial of glory to God in the Holy Eucharist and of reparation of all sacrileges and injuries committed against the Blessed Sacrament during the English Reformation'. Tongerlo Archives, E2 Engeland en Storrington', Box 1, 5/2. A Confraternity with the same dual orientation had been erected in November 1873 by mandate of Bishop Roskell.

26 *St Norbert's Parish Crowle. Centenary Booklet.* Muston Archives.

27 Tongerlo Archives, E2 Engeland en Storrington, Box 1, 5/1. On this figure, see Nigel Abercrombie, *The Life and Work of Edmund Bishop* (London: Longmans, 1959).

28 Letter of 11 January 1886 from Cardinal Newman to Martin Geudens, O.Praem. Tongerlo Archives, E2 Engeland en Storrington, Box 4, 19. The book in question was *Vita metrica sancti patris Norberti auctore Fratre Joanne Chrysostomo,*

Geudens's successor as prior of Crowle was a Dorset man, Matthew Smith (1859–1940), who ministered in the place for a remarkable forty-seven years, and, as was noted at the presentation for his leaving in 1930, had taken an interest in the people of the district well beyond the ranks of his own Catholic parishioners. He was, for example, secretary to the local branch of the National Society for the Prevention of Cruelty to Children.[29] It may not be too far-fetched to see that as an echo of the Tongerlo background. Pastoral practice in Flemish Catholicism was not that of a 'sect', such as English Catholic 'non-conformists' inevitably resembled. It was, rather, the sort of practice typical of a church of the nation, like the Church of England.

Whatever the merits, past and present, of the Norbertines considered as parish clergy, what the Tongerlo canons were engaged in founding, despite parochial (and educational) commitments, was patently a conventual institution. An 1878 rescript from the Congregation of Propaganda Fide, addressed to Edward Bagshawe (1829–1915), the third bishop of Nottingham, made clear that the usufruct of the mission was to belong to the canons, and not to the diocese.[30] And indeed the design of the new church at Crowle suggested as much. A long line of choirstalls separated the nave from a rather remote altar, leading the author of a survey commissioned by the Nottingham diocese in 2016 to remark, 'The church has a layout more typical of post-Tractarian Anglican churches than is usually found in Catholic churches, even in the 1870s'.[31]

The survey in question was chiefly concerned with artistic merit. Yet its context was more radical: expensive work on the fabric was needed, which raised the issue of sale for alternative use or even demolition (for which, however, opined the report's authors, the civil authority was unlikely to give permission). The canons had actually left a generation earlier, in 1983. The first Post-Reformation Lincolnshire priory was also the first (of two) to lose its position.[32]

That did not of course nullify the ministerial work of the past where chapels of ease had followed at two nearby villages. At Luddington, situated, like Crowle, in the Isle of Axholme, the patrons invoked were

abbate Tongerloënsi, O.Praem. (Namur: 1886). The letter itself is included in Francis J. McGrath, F. M. S. (ed.), *Letters and Diaries of John Henry Newman*, XXXII, Supplement (Oxford: Oxford University Press, 2008), pp. 471–2.

29 Gidney, *The Parish and Church of St Norbert's, Crowle,* p. 12.

30 Letter of 21 August 1878 from Congregation of Propaganda Fide to Edward Bagshawe. Muston Archives.

31 Nottingham Diocese, 'St Norbert, Fieldside, Crowle', originally archived 11 June 2016. Accessed 20 April 2023.

32 Gidney, *The Parish and Church of St Norbert's, Crowle,* p. 18.

St Joseph and St Dympna—the latter an interesting choice since the relics of the 'Lily of Éire' (doubtless the island of origin of some of the worshippers) are preserved not far from Tongerlo in the Belgian city of Geel, the place of her (seventh-century) martyrdom.

At Keadby, the terminus of the Stainforth to Keadby canal which passes through Crowle, a Catholic chapel was dedicated to Our Lady of Axholme—a reference to the pre-Reformation shrine of Melwood, which Premonstratensians had handed over to Carthusians in 1399. Pilgrimages to the site were a feature of Norbertine-inspired parish life in this district. Available land proved hard to find at Keadby. At the end of the 1950s Mass was still said in a room in a barber's shop—something reminiscent not only of the English Catholic Church in the Victorian countryside but even of the age of the Vicars Apostolic. But in late 1962 a little church able to seat a hundred folk was opened. Described by Kerigan, on behalf of the Crowle priory, as 'a neat little building of precast concrete, pebble dash, and with a barrel roof', it was paid for by the people of Crowle, Luddington, and Keadby in a common effort.[33] So much for the Isle of Axholme and North Holland generally.

In 1875, Spalding, in south Lincolnshire, tulip-producing country, became the first Tongerlo venture further afield.[34] It too was financed by Young, its church dedicated to 'The Immaculate Conception and St Norbert'. In July 1876 Frost and Dawson, 'Solicitors & Notaries' at Hull, sent the abbot of Tongerlo the draft deeds which put into his possession not only a substantial financial endowment by Thomas Young but also ownership of the lands and buildings both at Crowle and Spalding, finalized by a document of 11 July in the following year.[35] As at Crowle, Spalding was intended to have a conventual church equipped with choirstalls for canons at prayer. The first component of the patronal title—Immaculate Conception—suggests both the fervent devotion of the Norbertines of Brabant to the *diva Virgo candida*, and also alignment with the pontificate of Pius IX, still reigning, since he had dogmatized the relevant doctrine in 1854. Priory buildings and a schoolhouse were attached in the course of a three-year long process of construction.

But bricks were not everything. At Spalding, the Tongerlo canons had an agrarian tinge to their life, as appears from an undated obituary of one of their number, Frederick van Santen (1888–1920). Among

33 'Our Lady of Axholme is Back', *Catholic Herald* for 28 December 1962, p. 1.

34 Until 1875 the *Catholic Directory* for Great Britain described Spalding as served from Boston, where a church dedicated to St Mary dated from 1826: *The Catholic Directory, Ecclesiastical Register and Almanac for the Year of Our Lord 1875* (London: Burns, Oates, & Co., 1875), p. 184.

35 Tongerlo Archives, E2 Engeland en Storrington, Box 1, 1.

his responsibilities was a twenty-strong herd of cows and the brewing of ale—a predictable Belgian monastic speciality, though the canon in question had adopted British nationality.[36] In van Santen's time, if I interpret aright the relevant entries in the Muston Necrology, two Flemish priors spanned a half-century of governance. Thomas Aquinas van Biesen (1832–1908) held office as prior and parish priest between the year of foundation (1875) and 1903. His correspondence shows him to be a dedicated and responsible man, but hardly someone overjoyed by this long Lincolnshire assignment. Already in 1881 he was writing to Abbot de Swert, 'I will not refuse to remain longer in Spalding if this be your desire, but I must tell you that since some time I am rather disgusted with this place, and indeed I do not so much care for England as you seem to think'. Warning against a notion with which the abbot was evidently toying—the opening of a boarding school for Catholic boys, he added that 'Englishmen have a prejudice against Lincolnshire which they consider as very unhealthy'—perhaps surprising news to Late Victorian convalescents taking the sea-air at Cleethorpes or Skegness. In consequence, they would be unlikely to 'send their children to such a place as Spalding, the capital of the so dreaded Fens'.[37] Though eventually he came to terms with the Fenland and his long ministry was generally deemed a success, van Biesen thought Ireland the real place where canons of Tongerlo ought to be.[38] His pessimistic view of the prospects of the boarding school (which, on opening, managed to attract no more than ten pupils), and the viability of a convent of Norbertine Sisters (of whom only two actually took the veil),[39] was, however, swiftly borne out by events.

Van Biesen was followed at Spalding by an Antwerp man, Clement Tyck (1856–1950), who had been one of the original 'missionaries' in Tongerlo's Manchester venture, still to be described, and occupied the twin posts of prior and *parochus* amid the tulip-fields from 1903 to 1924. His musical gifts included the founding and direction of a highly successful 'Boys' Band'. These lengthy priorships, notably the latter, set their mark. Prior Tyck went from Spalding to be claustral prior of Tongerlo, a clear indicator of his mettle at a time when the canons of the abbey were numbered in hundreds—which is to say over two hundred.

In 1908 Spalding acquired, through Tyck's efforts, a Lourdes grotto:

---

36 *News Cuttings*, pp. 20–4. Muston Archives.

37 Letter of 11 September 1881 from Thomas Aquinas van Biesen, O.Praem., to Abbot de Swert. Tongerlo Archives, E2 England en Storrington, Box 1, 2/2.

38 Letter of 7 October 1879 from Thomas Aquinas van Biesen, O.Praem., to Abbot de Swert. Tongerlo Archives, E2 England en Storrington, Box 1, 2/2.

39 *The Immaculate Conception and St Norbert, Spalding, 1875–1975* (np, nd), p. 7. Tongerlo Archives, E2 Engeland en Storrington, Box 5, 38.

indeed, the priory was described as seeking to become the 'English Lourdes'.[40] The inference must be either that such garden shrines had not yet became commonplace in the grounds of Catholic chapels and churches or that this was preliminary to some more ambitious project—perhaps a copy to scale on the Welland of the famous Grotto on the Gave, rather as the Holy House of Walsingham (in Norfolk) was understood to replicate the Holy House of Loreto (on Italy's Adriatic coast). If so, one wonders what an historically Anglican town with a substantial minority of Protestant Dissenters would have made of it.[41] As the seat of the (early-eighteenth-century) 'Spalding Gentleman's Society', it would have given the membership, devoted to discussion of cultural, scientific, and antiquarian topics, an unusual subject for their lucubrations. In more than one sense the terrain was not well suited.

A parish history by Edward Fordham from the 1990s extracts a description of the inauguration of the sacred spot from Tyck's pamphlet, *The English Lourdes*:

> The Norbertine Abbot of Leffe [the temporary refuge of the canons of Frigolet, in exile again], a great admirer of the wonderful events at Lourdes, performed the Ceremony of the Blessing and sang the Pontifical Mass. Three o'clock was the appointed time for the more public ceremony of the Procession, which was marshalled by the Very Reverend Father [Philip] Fletcher, Master of the Guild of Ransom, who had also been the morning preacher … It was evident that all were struck at the earnestness and fervour of the processionists, especially of the Irish harvestmen, three hundred in number. The procession came to a standstill in Ayscoughfee Gardens, where Prior [Gilbert] Higgins spoke to five thousand people.[42]

The annual procession in honour of the Virgin of Lourdes was evidently a considerable event. A film of the 1913 procession is retained in the Lincolnshire Film Archive. The event took place each year till 1922, when a change of 'leading figures' led to its demise, though it was

---

40 Edward T. Fordham, *A History of the Catholic Church of the Immaculate Conception and St Norbert* (Spalding: no publisher, 1992), p. 3.

41 For the Spalding of this period, see Norman Leveritt and Michael J. Elsden, *Aspects of Spalding, 1790–1930* (Spalding: Chameleon, 1986).

42 Cited by Fordham, *A History of the Catholic Church of the Immaculate Conception and St Norbert*, pp. 3–4. I am grateful to Mr Michael Roberts of Spalding for kindly procuring for me a copy of this work. Philip Fletcher (1848–1928) was the first Master of the Guild of Ransom, in office from 1887 until his death. Gilbert Higgins, CRL, parish priest and prior of St Peter in Chains, Stroud Green, 1849–1940. In 1908 he had been made titular prior of Bridlington, a major house of his Order in mediaeval England, *Catholic Herald*, 22 November 1940, p. 7.

revived on a 'one-off' basis for centenary celebrations in 1975 to 1976.[43] One intriguing feature of the grotto site, which may account for the claims to uniqueness (the 'English Lourdes') is that it included a fixed erection, requiring heating in winter, rather than the expected outdoor arrangement: a duo of figures in a landscape.

As at Crowle, town boundaries had not limited the canons' apostolate. An item in a Muston scrapbook of 'News Cuttings' (the compiler is given as 'Th. Craig'[44]) records that during the period of seasonal labour by Irish 'harvesters', impromptu 'chapels' — improvised Mass-sites — were sought in a variety of barns and outbuildings in the Spalding district. These places were served by Norbertine priests cycling out from Spalding itself, accompanied by 'at least one altar server'.[45] Around 1910 the transport arrangements were facilitated by the loan of a horse and trap, and later, before the outbreak of the Second World War brought the system to an end, a motor car.[46] Attendance varied between an estimated 50 and 120 from site to site. The Dutch tulip- (and daffodil-) fields recreated on the English side of the North Sea were a major seasonal attraction for the under-employed or frankly unemployed.[47] Factoring in the 'Londoner' mission at Long Sutton, some thirteen miles east of Spalding, another work destination for flower-harvesters in the season, as many as 800 people were ministered to on a Sunday by Sunday basis in this unconventional fashion.[48] The oral tradition has it that Norbertine fathers (and brothers) of Dutch or Flemish origin were assigned for preference to Spalding owing to the large number of Dutch-speaking horticulturalists in the region.[49] A necrology composed at Muston by and large bears this out.

Against considerable opposition (indicative of warm attachment to the historic set-up), the original church and priory would be replaced in 2004 by new buildings, consisting of church, presbytery, and community hall. There was no place in such a scheme for the choirstall, the canon-regular's distinctive item of furniture. By this date the Norbertine

43 Fordham, *A History of the Catholic Church of the Immaculate Conception and St Norbert*, pp. 4, 9.

44 Presumably Thomas Craig, O.Praem, a canon of Tongerlo who subsequently left the Order to be incardinated as parish priest of Abbots Bromley in the diocese of Birmingham.

45 Fordham, *A History of the Catholic Church of the Immaculate Conception and St Norbert*, p. 21.

46 *Ibid.*

47 E. D. Turquand, 'The Lincolnshire Bulb Industry', *Scientific Horticulture* 23 (1971), pp. 67–74.

48 *News Cuttings*, p. 19. Muston Archives.

49 Conversation with Thomas Swaffer, O.Praem., Muston, 30 March 2023.

presence had shrunk from priory-scale to presbytery-sized, a prelude to the departure of the canons in 2008. St Norbert's school, integral to Young's scheme, had already outgrown its site several decades earlier. Looking back on the Lincolnshire missions from the vantage point of 1921, the *Spalding Guardian* recalled that Thomas Arthur Young 'with his four sisters [had] sold most of their possessions and lived in a cottage, in order to build Roman Catholic churches in Spalding, Crowle, Market Rasen, Gainsborough and Grimsby'. A batch of letters from Young to Geudens, chiefly on Crowle, in the Muston Archives, and a further set, from Young to van Biesen, chiefly on Spalding, in the Tongerlo Archives bear out claims to the assiduity of his accompaniment of Catholic and especially Norbertine expansion in Lincolnshire. A tell-tale sign of the economic cost is his admission to Geudens that it was 'most providential' for their plans that the foundations at Crowle and Spalding had preceded, but not by long, the agricultural crisis of the Late Victorian period—what Young himself roundly termed the 'collapse of farming'.[50]

That Young had found in Geudens a feisty priestly apologist as well as pastoral strategist was just as well. After Young's death (though no doubt also before it) critics had complained (the *Spalding Guardian* cited one such) that 'error will become propagated in the district and the blinding, delusive doctrines of a cruel and despotic Church become settled in our midst'. In its issue of 7 December 1875 (the Vigil of the Immaculate Conception—perhaps the date was not coincidental), the *Spalding Free Press* reminded readers in a leading article that 'The announcement in another column of the opening of a new Church in Spalding for the public and recognized worship of the Roman Catholic Church is one that gives us little surprise, though at the same time it is in our opinion an event which is very much to be deplored ... We commend therefore our townsmen to be wary of their wives and daughters, and the manhood of their sons, to stand shoulder to shoulder in obstructing its progress in the town.'[51] Martin Geudens took it upon himself to reply. The canons of Tongerlo had simply opened a small chapel where the same doctrine 'will be preached which your forefathers believed' and where the same sacraments 'will be administered which they received.' And Geudens concluded sardonically, 'What a dreadful crime!'.[52] Not all

50 Letter of 27 December 1886 from Thomas Arthur Young to Martin Geudens, O.Praem. Muston Archives. The period concerned has been defined as 1873 to 1896: T. W. Fletcher, 'The Great Depression of English Agriculture, 1873–1896', in P. J. Perry (ed.), *British Agriculture, 1875–1914* (London: Methuen, 1973), chapter 3.

51 Cited by Fordham, *A History of the Catholic Church of the Immaculate Conception and St Norbert*, p. 1.

52 'Local History XXXIV, The Catholics at Spalding', *Spalding Guardian*, 28 January 1921. Muston Archives.

local inhabitants were satisfied. From a vantage point some four miles to the east of Spalding, the vicar of Whaplode, the Reverend John Fairfax Franklin, applauded the paper's 'able and admirable leader'. He shifted the blame, however, from Roman Catholics, whether English, Irish, or Belgian, to the Anglo-Catholic party in the Church of England, those 'misguided pastors of our Protestant Church who by their Ritualistic ceremonies have so easily bridged over the great and wide gulf that exists between the Protestant Church of England and that of [sic] the Church of Rome'.[53]

Crowle and Spalding help to define the northern and southern edges, respectively, of the county of Lincoln. During the twentieth century, Tongerlo Norbertines expanded their efforts in both directions. Across the border into the West Riding of Yorkshire, activities at Stainforth, some seven miles to the north-east of Doncaster, and the starting-point of the canal link via Crowle to Keadby, followed in 1931. With Jerome Esser (1883–1948), a trained artist, as rector, the mission, or at any rate its church, Our Lady of the Assumption, profited from connexions to the world of art. The topic merits a paragraph of its own, not least because it belongs with a promising revival of the liturgical arts in the English Catholicism of its time.[54]

Esser was a canon of Tongerlo from Dutch Limburg, much travelled in the Indian sub-continent and the Levant, and prolific in various media: etchings, murals, oils, and water colours. The church and house were replete with his work, as well as that of the noted Anglo-Welsh artist Frank Brangwyn (1867–1956),[55] who had taught Esser at the Manchester School of Art. Brangwyn donated a notable set of Stations of the Cross to the Stainforth church in 1934, though it never received the publicity the Oxford Jesuits gave their parallel series (lithographs printed onto sycamore) at Campion Hall.[56] Esser's own style has been likened to that of the French Academician Pierre Puvis de Chavannes (1824–98), a sign that the Impressionist and Post-Impressionist movements had largely passed him by. Esser had also studied under Pierre Adolphe

---

53 Cited by Fordham, *A History of the Catholic Church of the Immaculate Conception and St Norbert*, p. 1.

54 Aidan Nichols, OP, *Artist and Monk. Dom Theodore Baily (1898–1966), Iconography and the Renewal of the Liturgical Arts in England* (Leominster: Gracewing, 2014).

55 Brangwyn had actually been born in Bruges, as a consequence of his father's move there after winning a competition organized by the (Belgian) Guild of St Thomas and St Luke for the best design of parish church: perhaps that was the initial link with Esser. See Rodney Brangwyn, *Brangwyn* (London: William Kimber, 1978).

56 They were reproduced as *The Way of the Cross. An Interpretation*, by Frank Brangwyn, R A, with a commentary by G. K. Chesterton (London: Hodder and Stoughton, 1935).

Vallette (1876–1942) who *was* an Impressionist, though the work of his best-known pupil, L. S. Lowry (1887–1976), suggests he did not always succeed in transmitting his aesthetic to others. Esser himself was closer to the Flemish artist Gerard Jacobs (1865–1978) who, together with his wife, Josephina Hendrickx, was the founder of 'Scheldt Luminism', exploring light effects but without loss of clarity of form. A delightful drawing from life of G. K. Chesterton (1874–1936)[57] in the Muston Archive *News Cuttings* is also reproduced in a study of the artist by V. Celen.[58] Esser's major works are reckoned as the fifteen scenes from the life of the Virgin at St Mary's Glossop, in the High Peak district of Derbyshire, and the companion ten scenes from the life of St Joseph in the chapel of a college at Weert, Esser's native place of birth. Among the Tongerlo missions, Esser also designed the stained glass for the east window at St Norbert's in Crowle.[59]

The Stainforth church, a low-ceilinged but otherwise traditionally conceived building in wood, was replaced by a consciously contemporary building, 'unfettered by adherence to artificial rules of symbolisms [*sic*]', in 1956.[60] In other words, it betokened the advent of the New Aniconicism associated with architectural Functionalism in its Catholic embodiment. John Carmel Heenan (1905–75), the fifth bishop of Leeds and later eighth archbishop of Westminster, approved the style but it fell to the abbot-general of the Premonstratensians to consecrate the result. The Brangwyn Stations of the Cross survived, and the building is said to have an excellent acoustic. Outside the liturgy, this Yorkshire parish, many of whose members were workers at the nearby Hatfield Colliery, was known for its sports teams, coached by a Tongerlo canon of Irish birth, Oliver Kelly, *parochus* from 1948 until his death (at some time after 1964, his silver jubilee of ordination[61]). Kelly, made a locum tenens on Esser's withdrawal through ill-health, had protested to Abbot Emiel Stalmans (1898–1953) that so Hibernian a parish needed an Irishman as its priest. Jerome Esser, claimed Kelly, had never understood the people: 'like the shamrock they will neither grow nor prosper outside

---

57 No mean draughtsman himself, and a critic of Impressionism to boot: Alzina Stone Dale, *The Art of G. K. Chesterton* (Chicago, IL: Loyola University Press, 1985).
58 *News Cuttings*, p. 74. Muston Archives. Cf. V. Celen, *Priester-Schilder Esser* (Turnhout: no publisher, nd), p. 79.
59 *News Cuttings*, pp. 69–81. Muston Archives.
60 'Church of the Assumption, Stainforth', in Parishioners of the Assumption, Stainforth, *Congratulations on the Silver Jubilee of the Very Rev. Fr. T. O. Kelly, CRP, PP* (Thorne: no publisher, 1964), no pagination. Muston Archives.
61 His absence from the Muston Necrology suggests that after the Belgian abbey's Irish daughter house, Kilnacrott, became an independent canonry (and, later, abbey) Kelly made a 'transitus' to there from Tongerlo.

an Irish atmosphere'.[62] Irish incomers would doubtless have become the Anglo-Irish by the time the Norbertines withdrew from the parish of Stainforth in 1984. The church, with its faults and merits, is now served from St Peter in Chains, Doncaster, part of the diocese of Hallam, itself newly formed in 1980 from areas of south Yorkshire and Lincolnshire in the circumscriptions of Leeds and Nottingham as marked out at the time of the restoration of the English and Welsh hierarchy in 1850.

Moorends, close to both Stainforth in the County of York and Thorne, in the County of Lincoln, had been since the 1890s the goal of Dutch Catholics immigrating in some numbers to work on the extraction of peat from the Moors.[63] After the Great War these Hollanders would be joined by Irish colliery workers in growing numbers. A mission was established from Crowle as early as 1896 when the prior of Crowle, Matthew Smith, was asked, with the permission of the Ordinary, William Gordon (second bishop of Leeds, 1831–1911), to 'take charge of the few catholics residing in Thorne and Stainforth'.[64] Here, unusually, the initiative was taken by secular clergy in the shape of the parish priest of St Peter's Doncaster, Charles Burke. Apart from the issue of pastors who could cope, directly or via *vlaams* with *nederlands* speech, there was some question of the eligibility of the aged in these small towns to obtain places in local 'resthomes' (care homes) if they remained attached more to Doncaster than to Crowle. A continuous presence of the canons was not achieved, however, till 1906, and even then Mass had to be celebrated in a school house (of the County rather than Catholic variety), this privilege owing to the useful connexions of a female parishioner with the West Riding County Council of which her husband was a member.[65] 'Not surprisingly, the majority of those baptized were Dutch children, right up to 1916, with an occasional Irish name appearing in the register.'[66] Perhaps by oversight, a canonically erected parish, belonging to the Premonstratensian Order, did not emerge until 1937. Church-building, belatedly begun at that date, continued till the start of the Second World War. The resultant parish church of Thorne-Moorends — dedicated to St Joseph and St Nicholas (the latter a popular figure in the Netherlands, especially in folklore) — was officially opened in 1939.

The Flemish links of this Tongerlo 'incorporated parish' were evidenced in the windows, by the glass artist Elfa Courtoit of Antwerp: in

---

62 Letter of 22 September 1948 from Oliver Kelly, O.Praem., to Abbot Stalmans of Tongerlo. Tongerlo Archives, E2 Engeland en Storrington, Box 5, 34.

63 [William Matthew Smith, O.Praem.], *St Joseph and St Nicholas, Moorends. Golden Jubilee, 1939–1989* (no place, no publisher, 1989), p. 3.

64 *Ibid.*

65 *Ibid.*, p. 4.

66 *Ibid.*, pp. 4–5.

the typological manner they showed, from the Old Testament prefigu-ration, Noah's ark, the crossing of the Red Sea, and the rock struck by Moses, and, for the New Testament fulfilment, the Baptism and saving Death of Christ.[67] A link with Stainforth continued, as was appropriate for fellow-Yorkshiremen, via the church primary school to which the parish of Thorne-Moorends made its due contribution in terms both of finance and pupils.[68] In 1987, a neat date, marking a half-century of service, the Moorends parish, following in the wake of its near-neigh-bour at Stainforth, was given into the care of the newly created Hallam diocese. Thus ended the Norbertine presence in the erstwhile West Riding of Yorkshire.

After World War II, one final Tongerlo parish was created. In the far south of Lincolnshire ('South Holland') Holbeach, where the church dedication is to the Holy Trinity, lies a mere eight miles from the Immac-ulate Conception and St Norbert at Spalding. It belongs, therefore, to bulb-producing country, vast amounts of which (some twenty thousand acres of fertile agricultural land), were salvaged from sea or marsh by efforts that, if they had begun in the early seventeenth century, continued into at least the 1830s. Beyond Holbeach, when starting from Spalding, lies the Wash, and the wetlands of Norfolk. Forming, accordingly, a natural appendix to the work of the Spalding priory, Holbeach was added to the cluster of Premonstratensian missions in 1956. On the withdrawal of the canons from Spalding, it was hardly likely that the Holbeach parish could retain its connexion with Prémontré. With the shrinking of the diocesan presbyterate, it is now served from Spalding, thus replicating the pattern of its own genesis. But by the same token the chapter of Lincolnshire re-implantation of St Norbert's Order had reached its conclusion. The shade of Thomas Arthur Young of Kingerby Manor will not have rejoiced.

In retrospect: successive abbots of Tongerlo appear to have enjoyed a relatively coherent concept of what they wished to achieve in the East of England. They wanted to establish a minimum kind of priory life on sites in market towns—specifically, Crowle and Spalding—each of which could count as the centre of an extensive rural district, the first moorland and agrarian (peat-cutting and flax-growing), and the second horticultural. From those bases it was feasible to set up a network of missions in villages that shared the economy, ethos, and immigration patterns of the surrounding countryside. It was a kind of scaled down version of the historic Norbertine model: an abbey with its 'incorpo-rated' parishes. That programme was assisted by the fact that, whether

67 *Ibid.*, p. 9.
68 *Ibid.*, pp. 11–12.

through expertise in the recovery of areas encroached on by the sea or by way of specialized knowledge of flower-growing, these rural areas in Lincolnshire and south Yorkshire already had a significant Dutch-speaking Catholic population, ministry among whom was easy for native speakers of Flemish. By a natural process of overspill, the north Lincolnshire missions, comparatively well-supplied with clergy, gained on the county border smallish quantities of industrial Yorkshire territory more perhaps by accident than by design.

Though as everywhere in what 'West Britons' would call 'The Mainland', Irish immigration, attracted by the labour opportunities of modern development, played, before the 1960s, an increasing part, the largely ruralist concept of the first, Mid-Victorian, Tongerlo implantation stands nonetheless in sharp contrast to the second wave—to what was attempted in Late Victorian Manchester. There Tongerlo would seek to do something very different in the Northern city which has the best claim to be the urban powerhouse of that Frankenstein monster, Britain's Industrial Revolution.

~ 4 ~

Dark Satanic Mills:
From Tongerlo to Manchester

THE CORPUS CHRISTI MISSION—possessed of a minor basilica, no less—in the northern English commercial capital of Manchester, dates from 1889. Abbot Heylen made this foundation at the request of Herbert Vaughan (1832–1903), second bishop of Salford and later the second archbishop of Westminster.[1] This was in sharp contrast to the lay initiative (albeit episcopally sanctioned) whereby Tongerlo canons came to eastern England. Vaughan's personal appeal was necessary. Something was being asked that lay well beyond the common experience of a Flemish abbey set in countryside worthy of the brush of Paul Bril (1554–1626) or Peter Paul Rubens (1577–1640). The canons were now invited to enter a commercial and industrial hub in order to serve a large and densely packed population, chiefly Irish or Irish-descended, of the kind that inspired Friedrich Engels to write—precisely in Manchester and Salford—his 1845 eye-opener *The Condition of the Working Class in England*.[2] According to the anonymous history of the community, produced for its centenary, at the time of its foundation there were in its assigned pastoral area some two and a half thousand nominal parishioners—largely, no doubt, Hibernian in origin and equally largely, by this date, unchurched.[3] It was not for nothing that, during the Christmas Octave of 1889, Vaughan wrote to Geudens, chosen for the leadership role: 'It will tax all your energy and will demand great self-sacrifice'.[4]

---

1 Ardura, *Premostratensi*, p. 401.
2 Friedrich Engels, *The Condition of the Working Class in England* (Oxford: Oxford University Press, 2009 [1845]), ed. David McLellan.
3 *Corpus Christi, Miles Platting, 1889–1989. The First 100 Years* (no place, no publisher, 1989), p. 2. Consulted in Salford Diocesan Archives, for access and help at which I am indebted to the archivist, Mr Paul Carr.
4 Letter of 29 December 1889 from Bishop Herbert Vaughan to Martin Geudens,

Martin Geudens, abandoning the Lincolnshire wheat fields, bought up the site of a disused glass factory in Varley Street, Miles Platting, a district lying north east of central Manchester along the Rochdale Canal. The Indenture made with 'the Reverend Louis Heylen and Others' on 20 December 1889 spoke of a 'plot of land, buildings and premises situate in Newton in the parish of Manchester in the County of Lancaster'.[5] There he began the building of a school which soon (in 1891) numbered 540 enrolled pupils,[6] as well as improvising conventual accommodation and a makeshift chapel for worship by the canons, both priests and brothers, he brought with him. The glass factory was undone: its ground floor showroom became the 'oratory', and its upper stories an architecturally bizarre 'priory'. This, then, was the unpromising conventual house of which Geudens was to become the first prior.

But perhaps one should write 'prior', in single inverted commas. Whether in eastern England or in Lancashire, officers of Geudens' sort were not conventual priors with full rights of governance (in the Norbertine vocabulary: priors 'de regimine'). Nor of course were they the claustral priors of an abbey with its own prelate. But a General Chapter at the Upper Austrian abbey of Schlägl in 1896 — the third of the modern sequence of General Chapters after the hiatus caused by the disappearance of the mother abbey of Prémontré in the Revolutionary turmoil — had authorized abbots to give the title 'prior' to local superiors (that is, priors of dependent houses) without, however, conceding right of attendance at those recently revived Chapters.[7] Crowle had been made such a 'priory', as was Spalding. But at the time the only other example, apart from Manchester, appears to have been the mission of the Dutch abbey of Berne at Rosiere Kewaunee, in the State of Wisconsin. Religious in small houses which scarcely differed in scale from the normal presbyteries of the secular clergy, and, like the latter, with parochial responsibilities to pursue, easily became indistinguishable (except by their dress) from diocesan clergymen, and Heylen's successor at Tongerlo, Abbot Cornelius Adrianus Deckers (1847–1915), thought it

O.Praem. Tongerlo Archives, E2 Engeland en Storrington, Box 3, 17.

5 Tongerlo Archives, E2 Engeland en Storrington, Box 1, 7.

6 *Corpus Christi, Miles Platting, 1889–1989. The First 100 Years*, p. 3. The 'rescue' of poor Catholic children from workhouses and schools that might threaten their faith was a major preoccupation of Vaughan during his later years (1881–92) as Bishop of Salford: see Robert O'Neil, MHM, *Cardinal Herbert Vaughan, Archbishop of Westminster, Bishop of Salford, Founder of the Mill Hill Missionaries* (Tunbridge Wells: Burns & Oates, 1975), pp. 271–6.

7 Leo C. Van Dijck, O.Praem., 'Les Chapitres généraux de l'Ordre au XIXe siècle: renaissance d'une institution', in Dauzet, Plouvier and Souchon, *Les Prémontrés au XIXe siècle*, pp. 175–92, and here at p. 189.

wise to produce a 'regula pro confratribus Angliae' outlining a schedule of life designed to put this particular confusion to rest.[8] 'Dependent' priory ought not to mean 'nominal' priory, in the sense of a house where the full Premonstratensian life was lived only in some quite token sense.

Geudens was not, however, just a prior. He was also, in due time, a titular abbot—the first of a series of such figures at Manchester. Their use of the *pontificalia*—mitre, crozier, ring, and gloves—gave a certain cachet to an Order which, in numerical terms, was by no means among the most significant in the Catholic Revival of the 'Second Spring'. (Norbertines do not figure, for instance, in the chapter on the revival of the masculine Religious Orders in the compendious volume on English Catholic life, 1850 to 1950, edited by the Assumptionist George Beck (1904–78), sixth archbishop of Liverpool, for the centenary of the restoration of the Hierarchy.[9]) One might recall that only with the 1899 Roman bull *Diu Quidem* did the priors of the long established English Benedictine houses of Downside, Ampleforth, and Douai become mitred abbots.[10] But as the instrument for the successful first implantation of modern Premonstratensians at Crowle a quarter of a century earlier, the honour of the title was a fitting tribute to Geuden's long experience of England, as well as to his parochial hard labour, above all in the singularly unpropitious circumstances (where beauty and comfort are concerned) of the south Lancashire of the industrial epoch. So it was that in 1898 Geudens became titular abbot of the pre-Reformation Lin-

---

8 *Regula pro Confratribus Angliae*, Tongerlo Archives ET, Engeland en Storrington, Box 2, 8. This 'regula' would reappear, with modifications, in 1922 and 1935 at the hands of Abbot Lamy, before becoming incorporated in 1939 into *Relicta Visitationis Canonicae apud Confratres Tongerloënses in Anglia*, promulgated jointly by Hubert Noots (1881–1967—he was originally a canon of Tongerlo) as Abbot-General and Emiel Stalmans as abbot of Tongerlo. Tongerlo Archives, E2 Engeland en Storrington, Box 5, 30. At Frigolet an undated document entitled *Des religieux en mission*, possibly from the abbacy of Paulin Boniface, when the issue first became relevant there, carries a similar message to the Tongerlo *regula*. Frigolet Archives, Cartons Storrington, E28.

9 George Andrew Beck, AA (ed.), *The English Catholics 1850–1950. Essays to commemorate the centenary of the restoration of the hierarchy of England and Wales* (London: Burns & Oates, 1950).

10 For a brief account of the struggle over the restoration of autonomous abbeys in a Congregation previously ruled by a President-General assisted by two Provincials (the latter till 1889, after which the 'missions' in England were placed under conventual priors), see Bernard Green, OSB, *The English Benedictine Congregation: A Short History* (London: Catholic Truth Society, 1980). Before the French Revolution there was one exception—but it was in Germany: Anselm Cramer, OSB (ed.), *Lamspringe: An English Abbey in Germany, 1643–1803*, Saint Laurence Papers VII (Ampleforth: Ampleforth Abbey, 2003).

colnshire abbey of Barlings.[11]

It seems worth asking, Why that particular choice? The mediaeval abbey was not in the immediate neighbourhood of a modern Norbertine parish. It may have been selected in the hope that its last abbot, Matthew Makkarell (died 1537), and his six companions, all of whom were executed at Tyburn for resistance to the Henrician Reformation, might at some future date be declared *beati* by the Catholic Church.[12] That was not out of the question, but the timing of the Lincolnshire Rising, in its relation to the Pilgrimage of Grace, rendered their witness rather ambiguous. At what point did religious resistance become political opposition?[13] The English Dominican historian Walter Gumbley (1887–1968), wrote a short position paper, 'Martyrs or Traitors?', for the benefit of the Norbertines at Crowle, in which he put the case for the former category. Presumably unpublished, a copy is preserved both in the Muston Archives and at Tongerlo. 'It is noticeable', wrote Gumbley, 'in the indictment of these Pilgrims that the first and principal charge against them was that "they maliciously and by diabolical instigation conspired to attempt to deprive the King's Grace of his title and dignity of supreme head on earth of the Church in England". The other vague charges as to unlawful assemblies, taking up arms, of thoughts, and words and deeds against their prince, etc., etc., were put in for fear the jury *per impossibile* would find the main charge not proven.'[14] The Holy See, however, has been too prudent (not necessarily in the Aristotelian sense) to accept the Gumbley thesis.

The other key figure in the establishment of the Manchester priory was a Tongerlo canon of English birth, John Gerebern Seadon (1856–1930). Born in Birmingham, he received the habit at Tongerlo in 1873 (his Religious name is that of St Dympna's confessor who was included in her cultus in Flanders, the scene of her martyrdom). By 1880 he had returned home and ministered at Spalding before going to the newly

---

11 On the mediaeval abbey, see Colvin, *The White Canons in England*, pp. 70–7, and, much more fully, Paul Everson and David Stocker, *Custodians of Continuity? The Premonstratensian Abbey at Barlings and the Landscape of Ritual* (Sleaford: Heritage Trust of Lincolnshire, 2011).

12 W. A. J. Archbold, 'Makkarell or Mackarell, Matthew', in *Dictionary of National Biography* (London: Smith, Elder, & Co., 1885–1900), vol. XXXV, *s.v.*; Margaret Bowker, 'Mackarell (Makkarell), Matthew', *Oxford Dictionary of National Biography*, vol. XXXV (New York: Oxford University Press, 2004), pp. 494–5. Makkarell and his companions had been included among the Order's martyrs in seventeenth-century accounts.

13 See R. W. Hoyle, *The Pilgrimage of Grace and the Politics of the 1530s* (Oxford: Oxford University Press, 2001), where the material for Lincolnshire is discussed on pp. 93–134.

14 Walter Gumbley, OP, 'Martyrs or Traitors?', p. 2. Muston Archives

opened Corpus Christi priory in 1889. He would succeed Geudens as parish priest and regular superior and, eventually, as titular abbot likewise.[15]

The Miles Platting parish, led by these dependent priors who were simultaneously titular abbots, offered a wide variety of services over and above the sacramental or liturgical ministrations that, in a church setting, come immediately to mind. A 'night school', the Corpus Christi Continuing Education School, providing an extension of education for adults, chiefly in technical domestic and commercial subjects, was one of only three in Manchester. It was a remarkable achievement to have established such a going concern in one of the city's bleakest and most impoverished areas.[16] Confraternities and guilds, such as those dedicated to Blessed Hermann Joseph (*c.* 1150–1241), the Rhenish mystic, or to the virgin martyr St Agnes (291–304), or the more commonly found 'Children of Mary' provided a niche form of sociality, as did the distinctive 'Third Order of St Norbert'.[17] A brass band achieved celebrity even in a city and region where competition among such music-makers was intense.[18] The annual Corpus Christi summer fetes, imaginatively multi-activity affairs, were long remembered.[19]

Fund-raising for an ambitiously conceived basilican church continued for some forty years. Perhaps uniquely, the papal document erecting a 'Votive Basilica' preceded not only the completion of the building but the inception of the building-work, dated as it was to 17 May 1904. Building-work on the nave began in 1906. Work on the sanctuary and the portion of the nave nearest the sanctuary was deliberately postponed, while a tower intended to complete the edifice was never erected. The doubly truncated church was officially opened on 5 December 1907. The reason for the unlikely privilege (status of a minor basilica) accorded a church that was at the time purely theoretical lay in the purpose for which the proposed building was destined: an intenser cultus of the Eucharistic sacrament, itself a principal preoccupation of the occupation of the chair of Peter by Pope Pius X (1835–1914).

Approximately half-way through the period of construction, an appeal by Louis Charles Casartelli (1852–1925), the fourth bishop of Salford, writing from St Bede's College, of which he had become the Rector in 1891, spoke of the sacrifice English and Belgian (or Dutch) canons had made in coming to Miles Platting. 'Leaving their beautiful

15 *News Cuttings*, pre-pagination pages. Muston Archives.
16 *Corpus Christi, Miles Platting, 1889–1989*, p. 9.
17 *Ibid.*, p. 5.
18 *Ibid.*
19 *Ibid.*, p. 8.

and salubrious old abbey of Tongerloo [sic], they settled down in one of the dreariest and most depressing spots in this vast, ever growing city.'[20] The combination of mills, chemical- and gas-works, and a tannery certainly did not make for healthy living. By the middle of the following century, with industrial degeneration, the area would be regarded as one of the worst slums in Britain if not in Europe. From the start, the canons in residence had to set their sights resolutely by supernatural stars. Ten years after the initial purchase, the *Catholic Herald* saluted the new Mancunian enterprise when reporting a fund-raising event in the time of the third bishop, John Bilsbarrow (1836–1903): 'The first and special efforts of the new missioners were directed towards rescuing Catholic children from Protestant schools and of special devotion to the Blessed Sacrament'.[21]

The latter was a reference, no doubt, not simply to the strongly Eucharistic ethos the Order of Prémontré had derived from its founder, but also to the 'Archconfraternity of the Mass of Reparation' which Geudens initiated in his adopted country. The idea of Rose of Bonlieu (Louise-Madeleine-Euphrosine Mirabal, 1812–82), a Parisian lay-sister with a claim to beatification, it was a response to de-Christianization in France and lapsation elsewhere.[22] Members promised to attend an additional Sunday Mass in order to 'repair' for the absence of the hostile or indifferent. It became for a while a distinctive Norbertine cause, and at its height attained a total membership of over a million. At the (world) Eucharistic Congress held at Namur in 1902 Geudens had made a report on the introduction into Britain and Ireland of the *Archiconfrèrie de la Messe réparatrice*, with an organizing centre at Miles Platting. Though a characteristically nineteenth-century conception, it was part and parcel of his wider Premonstratensian *pietas*. A newspaper obituary of 18 July 1913 hailed Geudens as the 'pioneer of the English Norbertines', who appropriately enough died on St Norbert's day that year.[23]

Something of a flurry of newspaper interest attended the appointment of his successor, simply because Seadon was the first Englishman since the Middle Ages to be blessed as an abbot in the Norbertine Order. In April 1901 Prior Seadon was installed as abbot of Welbeck, a twelfth-century foundation in the dukeries of North Nottinghamshire and now the residence of the dukes of Portland.[24] In 1512, the abbots

20 *News Cuttings*, pre-pagination pages. Muston Archives.
21 'Bazaar at Miles Platting. Sketch of Corpus Christi Mission. History of the White Canons', *Catholic Herald*, 15 September 1899, p. 13. Muston Archives.
22 Arthur Loth, *Sister Rose: Her Life and Work and the Mass of Reparation*, translated by Martin Roestenburg, O.Praem. (Waterloo, ON: Arouca Press, 2021).
23 *News Cuttings*, pre-pagination pages. Muston Archives.
24 A. Hamilton Thompson, *The Premonstratensian Abbey of Welbeck* (London:

of Welbeck had been given authority over all the Premonstratensian houses in England—part of the struggle between the English crown and 'mother-houses' overseas whither, to the disapproval of the English treasury, money left the country in the form of taxation by General Chapters or by the abbots of Prémontré. In that context, the choice of title rather suggests Seadon hoped he would live to see a plurality of not only abbots but abbeys in the English revival of the Order—alas, a very vain hope indeed. Assisted by the abbots of Tongerlo and Parc (the latter is situated in Louvain), he received the abbatial blessing from John Stephen Vaughan (1853–1925), Casartelli's auxiliary, and brother to Cardinal Vaughan. (Casartelli himself, as the newspaper accounts reported, was not cooling in his support: he had only been indisposed.[25]) The Muston *News Cuttings* volume contains pieces by the *Daily News and Leader*, the *Daily Despatch*, and the *Daily Sketch*, as well as from regional papers (the *Manchester Evening News* and *Manchester Evening Chronicle*) as well as, more predictably the *Catholic Times*.[26] The pre-Conciliar Catholic Church knew how to do these things with a great deal of pomp and circumstance that, at any rate, brought dignity and a splash of colour into the grey, not to say grime-blackened, landscape of a major industrial as well as commercial city.

Corpus Christi basilica, a building modelled on the Italian Romanesque, would only be completed in 1938 with the creation of a sanctuary in Byzantine style floored in Lancashire marble though with a high altar in the Belgian marble that suited its Tongerlo origins. Appropriately enough, the designer of the completed architectural plan, a certain Léon Lamy, was the blood-brother of an abbot of Tongerlo.

By that date, the eve of renewed war in Europe, the parish priest was George Toner (1874–1948), born in Manchester, clothed at Tongerlo in 1893, and appointed assistant priest in Spalding in 1899 from where he had returned to his native city in 1902. In 1932 he became Seadon's successor. He would be the last of the titular abbots in Manchester when in January 1934 he was ceremonially blessed by Thomas Henshaw (1873–1938), fifth bishop of Salford and a product of Miles Platting. He took the title abbot of Cockersand or 'St Mary's in the Marsh', a rather inaccessible site by Morecambe Bay, between the estuaries of the Wyre and the Lune, on the historic boundary between the hundreds of Fylde and Lonsdale.[27] A Lancastrian himself, he had taken an active interest

Faber and Faber, 1938); Colvin, *The White Canons in England*, pp. 63–70.

25 For more on Seadon's enthronement, see *News Cuttings*, pp. 1–15. Muston Archives.

26 *News Cuttings*, pre-pagination pages. Muston Archives.

27 Colvin, *The White Canons in England*, pp. 138–43; Brian Marshall, *Cockersand*

in the work of excavation and preservation in that exposed and (in the mediaeval period) remote location. Toner had been the first postulant at St Norbert's in Crowle in 1891, so he had, at various times, experience of all three of the Tongerlo 'priories' to date (Crowle, Spalding, Manchester). He was evidently the subject of the letter of 27 November 1871 from John Philips to Abbot de Swert, written from 7 Orchard Street, Portman Square, which mentioned as a 'charming boy ... our little English postulant' who has 'set himself to learn Latin', being as he was 'still keen to embrace Religious life'.[28] Extant photographs of Toner in full pontificals (there is one at Our Lady of Sorrows Priory in Peckham) bear out the report on his small stature, so the diminutives are not necessarily those of affection.

He was the last of the titular abbots at Manchester; his successor, Anselm Cross (1887–1982), a Prestonian, had to be content, on becoming, in 1948, parish priest, with the title 'Regular Superior of the English Mission'. For it was the case—and this should perhaps have been mentioned earlier—that the 'abbatial' character of the 'titular' figures at Manchester had not been purely a matter of antiquarian enthusiasm or ceremonial display. Each in turn was responsible, subject to the yea or nay of the Prelate at Tongerlo, for the deployment of personnel among the priories (including, after its foundation, the Irish house of Kilnacrott) and in the incorporated parishes.

During the Second World War, when Toner was superior, the priory (still at that time the two top floors of the old glass works—though an ambitious building scheme for an abbey on the traditional model was ultimately in mind), sustained considerable damage from the effects of the Manchester Blitz, as did likewise the school and church.[29] In the later 1950s, a simple set of modern buildings (both priory and hall) could easily be erected as a temporary measure—and was—until such time as an abbey, for which the land was available, could be attempted. But the church, already one of the largest Catholic parish churches in England (and the first 'minor basilica', preceding in that respect the far better-known abbey church of Downside), was another matter. Though holes were filled, continuing weaknesses in the roof of the basilica were noted as early as 1950.[30] Meanwhile, post-war rehousing of the population was reducing the parish population—and Mass attendance—by

Abbey. A Lancashire House of Premonstratensian Canons, 1180–1539 (Staining: Landy Publishing, 2001).

28 Letter of 27 November 1871 from John Philips to the abbot of Tongerlo. Muston Archives.

29 *Corpus Christi, Miles Platting, 1889–1989*, p. 11.

30 *Ibid.*, pp. 12–13.

some forty per cent.[31] With that reduction came a corresponding dim-
inution in income. When in 1961 the collapse of part of the floor in the
parochial hall required the latter's demolition it was an ominous sign
of things to come. Fast forward by fifty years (or less), and the basilica
had become irreparable except at the cost of an expenditure of millions,
quite beyond the capacities of a poor parish to generate.[32]

The day was not at hand when the neighbourhood, at any rate in
significant part, would be regenerated—indeed, lined with boutique
dwellings—in a Manchester which, at the time of writing (2023), is
reputed to be Europe's fastest growing city. The last prior *de regimine*
at Miles Platting, Michael Gallagher (born 1931),[33] has computed that
over the 117 years of their presence at Corpus Christi, the basilica—
and the priory and parish life of which it was the hub—have inspired
some fifty-seven vocations to the Religious life for women and over
thirty vocations to the priesthood, whether secular or regular.[34] Even
if the effects on the lives of the laity are beyond the historian's ability to
quantify, by this vocational marker alone that was no trivial outcome
to a Victorian encounter between a bishop of Salford and an abbot of
Tongerlo.

On that note I shall leave for now the canons stemming from the
Belgian abbey so as to consider the other prong of the modern British
Premonstratensian fork, which is not Flemish but French

---

31 *Ibid.*, p. 13.

32 'Landmark church closes', *Manchester Evening News*, 30 April 2007. Salford
Diocesan Archives.

33 'Last prior *de regimine*': he was followed by Hugh Allan, O.Praem., as prior
administrator.

34 Estimates based on entries of profession and ordination in baptismal records
provided by Michael Gallagher, O.Praem., in a conversation of 9 June 2023. The
records may be consulted, for the early period, in the Lancashire County Archives in
Preston, or for the later period at St Patrick's, Livesey Street, Collyhurst, Manchester.

～ 5 ～

Provence in Exile:
The Frigolet Background

T HE ABBEY OF FRIGOLET had a distinctly unusual start, entirely bound up with the biography of its founder, or rather re-founder, Jean-Baptiste (in religion, Edmond) Boulbon (1817–83), a monk of the Cistercian abbey of Notre-Dame de Gard near Amiens, from where this Trappist community decamped in 1845 to become the abbey of Sept-Fons in the Bourbonnais.[1] Edmond Boulbon had proved an extremely successful fundraiser in this expensive process, so much so that he became a professional preacher-fundraiser for various Cistercian projects, of which the last and least successful was an attempted Trappist foundation on the Ile Bourbon in the Indian Ocean (now 'Réunion'). But his spirituality was taking on an increasingly liturgical cast, with an emphasis on the doxological character of the rites. The liturgy, he thought, should be celebrated sumptuously—rather a difficulty for those in a Cistercian tradition whose historic mentality was defined in part by opposition to the elaborately ritual monasticism of the Black Monks of Cluny.

But then an opportunity presented itself.[2] In 1855 the bishop of Soissons, Paul-Armand Cardon de Garsignies (1803–60) acquired what remained of the arch-abbey of Prémontré. He proposed a collaboration: the energetic and efficient as well as visionary Boulbon should restore the abbey and with it the Premonstratensian Order in France, thus enabling him to combine Cistercian austerity of life with Cluniac

---

1 For his life, see Bernard Ardura, 'Biographie du Père Edmond Boulbon', in his (ed.) *Création et tradition à Saint-Michel de Frigolet* (Frigolet: Abbaye Saint-Michel, 1984), pp. 9–20; Ardura, *L'Abbaye Saint-Michel de Frigolet*, pp. 199–224.

2 Bernard Ardura, 'Les Tentatives de restauration de l'Ordre de Prémontré en France au XIXe siècle', in Guy Bedouelle (ed.), *L'Acordaire. Son pays, ses amis et la liberté des ordres religieux en France* (Paris: Cerf, 1991), pp. 265–89; for the history of Frigolet more widely, see Ardura, *L'Abbaye Saint-Michel de Frigolet*, pp. 23–196.

liturgical extravagance. It seems unlikely that the bishop explained he had simultaneously invited the canons of Tongerlo to purchase the abbey from the diocese for a somewhat exorbitant sum. Combined with the importation of Daughters of Wisdom to run the place as an orphanage, that discovery led, not surprisingly, to Boulbon's precipitate withdrawal — in the habit of the Order with which the bishop, by a certain *insouciance*, had already clothed him.

But Boulbon retained the idea of a Norbertine restoration. On a cue from Jean-Marie Vianney, the Curé d'Ars (1786–1859), he found a suitable alternative property, a former abbey of Augustinian canons at Frigolet in Provence: in the wonderful countryside of the Montagnette, not far from the Pont du Gard. It was a good choice not only for its natural beauty (though in recent times, specifically in the summer of 2022, it has been ravaged by an out-of-control forest fire). This was *la Vendée provençale*, an area that had long sought to resist the Revolution. It could be expected that well-wishers in some numbers — and, for that matter, Norbertine vocations — might be found there. More widely, Boulbon's large circle of acquaintances, which included the eminent bishop of Orleans Félix-Antoine-Philibert Dupanloup (1802–78), the (Roman) Secretary of the Congregation for Regulars and later cardinal Frédéric de Falloux du Coudray (1815–84), and the Legitimist pretender to the throne of France, M. le Comte de Chambord, to his numerous followers Henri V (1820–83), gave him the contacts and influence that made the project viable.

Rather than adopting the then current (seventeenth-century) Premonstratensian Statutes, Boulbon obtained a copy of the 1290 Statutes of the Order which he (wrongly) believed to be the Primitive Rule, and gained the sanction of Pius IX for the establishment of a 'Primitive Observance of Prémontré', under the supervision of the local bishop (who was archbishop of Aix-en-Provence), but with himself as the first Superior, duly empowered to receive the profession of future Religious. In a scheme which could justly be called grandiose (and some have used the harsher term 'megalomaniac'), Boulbon had acquired a Romanesque church of the twelfth century, dedicated to St Michael, a cloister of the same period, and a number of conventual buildings, admittedly in deplorable condition, as well as a goodly haul of ruins. He set about the transformation of the entire site, hugely extending the buildings and erecting a magnificent *abbatiale*, a twin-spired and elaborately decorated church in honour of the Immaculate Conception (the extraordinary events at Lourdes, where the Mother of God announced herself under that title, were of recent occurrence), with a subsidiary dedication to St Joseph. On the north side of the church a neo-Romanesque chapel aimed to continue an ancient local devotion to 'Our Lady of Good Remedy',

Notre-Dame-du-Bon-Remède.[3]

In 1861 Boulbon established a boys' choir to add lustre to the liturgical celebrations. Its school was something of a pioneer when in 1872 it adopted the polyphony of Giovanni Pierluigi da Palestrina (1525–94) as the model for its music, thus anticipating the work of Sir Richard Terry (1864–1938) at London's Westminster Cathedral. But his ambitions did not stop there. In 1868 Pius IX had declared the Frigolet priory the *domus princeps* of a 'Congregation of the Primitive Observance of Prémontré', and subsequently demonstrated his favour once again by raising the priory to the status of an abbey. Abbot Boulbon (as Père Edmond thus became) did not enjoy the support of the succeeding archbishop of Aix, but he managed nevertheless to make a number of new foundations, none of which, however, was to endure, with the sole exception of Saint-Foi de Conques, in the Aveyron—though in due course this passed into the hands of Frigolet's northern competitor, the Norman abbey of Mondaye. It sometimes seems there are two Frances, divided by the Loire.

Not unfriendly bishops but the anti-clerical politics of the Third French Republic threatened entirely to undo Boulbon's work. In 1880, leaning on the undoubted juridical fact that few if any of the 'Congregations' of Catholic Religious were legally established, the Government declared dissolved first the Jesuits and then a further three hundred or so Religious institutes or autonomous houses on French soil. Among them was Frigolet in whose case a company of dragoons was dispatched to deal with the recalcitrance of both the canons and the choristers, Boulbon remaining on the premises as the legal owner.

Dying in the deserted abbey, he was succeeded in 1883 as Superior General of the Congregation of the Primitive Observance and simultaneously abbot of Frigolet by Paulin Boniface (1853–1927), a vital, if controversial, figure in the return of Premonstratensians to the British Isles. For Abbot Boniface, recommended by Boulbon to Leo XIII for approval *ad nutum Sanctae Sedis*—owing to the dispersion of the canons no abbatial election was possible, proved to be a stormy petrel.[4]

Some further consideration will be given below to the subsequent history of the abbey under the heading 'From Frigolet to Tongerlo' (Chapter 9). But here I turn without further ado to the veritable diaspora of foundations Frigolet's second abbot authorized in the dramatic circumstances of enforced exile.

---

3 For the origins of this devotion among Trinitarian friars (*Ordo Sanctissimae Trinitatis et Captivorum*), see Ardura, *Au cœur de la Provence. L'abbaye saint-Michel de Frigolet* (Rome: no publisher, 2000), pp. 19–24. The purse ('remedy') held out to the Madonna by the Holy Child is the ransom money for Christian captives.

4 Ardura, *L'Abbaye Saint-Michel de Frigolet*, pp. 44, 47–9, 51–5.

～ 6 ～

A Sussex Idyll:
From Frigolet to Storrington

WHEN THE FRIGOLET CANONS considered the possibility of an English foundation as a safe harbour during turbulent times in France,[1] they were fortunate to encounter Henry Fitzalan-Howard, the fifteenth Duke of Norfolk (1847–1917), a devout and generous benefactor to the English Catholic Church up and down the land.[2] Indeed, he 'devoted the largest part of his income throughout his life to the support of the Catholic Church in England, building cathedrals, churches and schools, subsidizing hospitals, convents, seminaries, as well as most charitable causes and an unknown number of private individuals in distress'.[3] In Paris the Ultramontane propagandist Louis Veuillot's (1813–83) newspaper *L'Univers* reported on an announcement in London's *Morning Post*. The Duke of Norfolk had offered the equivalent of three hundred thousand francs for the foundation of a new episcopal see in Sussex on condition that it incorporated the name of his seat, Arundel, and a further equivalent of twenty thousand francs for acquiring a terrain 'propitious to the foundation of a monastery to which a new parish could be attached'. Paulin Boniface, now Superior General, was struck by the discovery. He had been 'preoccupied with the lot of Religious Orders and the future in France of our Congregation which events threaten more and more', and 'understood that Providence was coming quickly to his help'.[4] Henry Norfolk wrote to him on 29 December 1881, 'I write to make a formal offer to your Fathers

---

1 For their first expulsion from Frigolet, under the anti-clerical legislation of 1880, see Ardura, *Au cœur de la Provence*, pp. 79–81.

2 See John Martin Robinson, *The Dukes of Norfolk* (Chichester: Phillimore, 1995, 2nd edition), pp. 212–35.

3 *Ibid.*, p. 212. On his role at Storrington, see H. M. Gillett, *[The] Shrine of Our Lady of England at Storrington* (Exeter: Catholic Records Press, 1954), p. 4.

4 Louis de Gonzague Daras, *Fondation d'Angleterre*, p. 2. Muston Archives.

of the land at Storrington, subject to the conditions agreed upon and to the approval of the Bishop of the [Southwark] Diocese'.[5] Travelling to London to visit first the bishop and then the duke, who had only recently, in 1879, acquired the lordship of the manor of Storrington (though the land concerned had been an historic Howard possession), Abbot Boniface inspected the site and found the climate 'gentle, pure and salubrious', and the proximity to the 'ancient and charming city of Arundel' a distinct advantage. He was told that Catholic parishes founded by émigré clergy had done well, and noted how the Carthusians of the Grande Chartreuse were preparing for their expulsion by building a new monastery (St Hugh's Charterhouse) at nearby Parkminster.

Somewhat optimistically, Louis de Gonzague Daras (1820–92),[6] author of the Memoir drawn on here, opined that 'the Catholic religion is marvellously respected throughout this kingdom, and the very recent official receptions of cardinals of England at royal audiences and in the counsels of Queen Victoria [1819–1901] is a peremptory proof of it'.[7] This would doubtless have been a surprise to Victoria R. I. He waxed lyrical about the number of pre-Reformation English Premonstratensian houses whose names appeared in William Dugdale's (1605–86) classic *Monasticon Anglicanum*,[8] claiming (almost certainly incorrectly) that the only pope England produced, Adrian IV (*c.* 1100–59), was a Norbertine canon.[9]

The Daras Memoir ended by recording that on 22 January, 1882, a group of Frigolet canons left Tarascon-sur-Rhône, their nearest town, travelling at the expense of a Paris-based 'Committee of Succour to

---

5 Letter of 29 August 1881 from the Duke of Norfolk to Abbot Paulin Boniface. Frigolet Archives, Cartons Storrington, E28.

6 On this figure, see Ardura, *L'Abbaye Saint-Michel de Frigolet*, pp. 227–8. For his writings, see André Léon Goovaerts, *Ecrivains, artistes et savants de l'Ordre de Prémontré. Dictionnaire bio-bibliographique* (Brussels: Société belge de librairie, 1899–1916), I., pp. 539–42.

7 Louis de Gonzague Daras, *Fondation d'Angleterre*, p. 2. Muston Archives

8 Originally written in Latin during the Protectorate and in the early years of the Restoration, between 1655 and 1673, the work was published posthumously in English in 1693 with the sub-title 'The History of the Ancient Abbies [sic], and other Monasteries, Hospitals, Cathedral and Collegiate Churches in England and Wales. With Divers French, Irish, and Scotch Monasteries formerly relating to England'; the edition to which Daras had access is probably that published at London by Bohm in 1846.

9 The older Norbertine genealogies do indeed make this claim, through a seeming misinterpretation of a phrase in a letter by Adrian IV to a Premonstratensian abbot. A much more likely twelfth-century candidate is Alberto di Morra, elected in 1154 as Gregory VIII: see Basil R. Reuss, 'A Norbertine Pope?', *Catholic Historical Review* 19/2 (1933), pp. 200–2.

Expelled Religious', and on 2 February, feast of the Purification, having landed on English soil at Newhaven, the small party duly arrived at Storrington.[10] Apart from Daras himself, they consisted of a deacon, a cleric, a postulant, and a lay brother.[11] They were accommodated originally in borrowed housing at Sand Lodge, on School Hill, while they looked around as to how their implantation might best be effected. This happy landing was indebted in part to the efforts Norfolk's remote cousin Edward Henry Howard (1829–92), cardinal priest of SS Giovanni e Paolo, and later bishop of Frascati,[12] had made by way of encouragement of the project,[13] which was also approved by the exiled and widowed Eugénie (1826–1920), Empress of the French. Howard, whose imposing presence and military voice struck fear into Italian sacristans in the course of his arch-priestly duties at the Vatican Basilica, was a notable ally, especially since as Protector of the English College he was likely to be consulted on ecclesiastical matters concerning England. So the founding went ahead, with considerable enthusiasm from the Frigolet side. 'There is a community to establish, a monastery to organize, schools to form, orphans to gather, poor folk to help, vocations to promote, land to cultivate and above all souls in great number to save.'[14]

Those aims are fully congruent with a compendious document produced to advertise the ducal foundation, several copies of which are preserved in the Frigolet Archives. There the 'works of the Religious' were given as 'a mission of 12 to 15, 000 souls where there are but few Catholics, the creation of a monastery, a novitiate, an orphanage, and the building of a church.' Objects necessary for the cult were singled out for especially urgent attention (the party from Frigolet did not even have a tabernacle in which to house the reserved Sacrament). Spiritual benefits, some intangible, others less so, were promised in return. Mass and Vespers were sung daily in perpetuity for benefactors. An image of Our Lady of England on Bristol paper would be sent to each benefac-

10 Louis de Gonzague Daras, *Fondation d'Angleterre*, p. 3. Muston Archives.

11 Unsigned Memoir entitled *Storrington 1882–1982*, p. 1. Muston Archives. The lay brother was, presumably, Cuthbert Johnson (1842–1904), buried at Storrington.

12 See on this figure Nicholas Schofield and Gerard Skinner, *The English Cardinals* (Oxford: Family Publications, 2007), pp. 157–9.

13 Howard had visited Frigolet while a deacon and conceived a great admiration for Boulbon, see Ardura, *L'Abbaye Saint-Michel de Frigolet*, p. 47, who refers to Peter Cassidy, 'La Fondation du Prieuré Notre-Dame d'Angleterre à Storrington', in Ardura, *Création et tradition à Saint-Michel de Frigolet*, pp. 95–8, and here at p. 95.

14 Louis de Gonzague Daras, *Fondation d'Angleterre*, p. 2. Muston Archives. A *lettre circulaire* was addressed to all his Religious by Paulin Boniface explaining the circumstances and aim of the foundation. The text is found in Ardura, *L'Abbaye Saint-Michel de Frigolet*, pp. 525–7.

tor donating a minimum of one franc, while a copy of the (illustrated) 'Diploma of Foundation' would be dispatched to those giving twenty-five francs or more.[15]

The enthusiasm was by no means wholly displaced. Nor were the entreaties for help entirely fruitless. The Church historian Martin Gillett described Storrington as 'splendidly situated ... with open views of the South Downs and Charltonbury Hill'.[16] Dedicated to Our Lady of England, who was represented by a Tyrolean statue in wood above the high altar, the work of Ferdinand Stüflesser (1855–1926),[17] the priory's Marian holdings included a copy of the Stroganov School Procopius Chirin's (d. 1621) Vladimir icon given by Leo XIII on the fiftieth anniversary of his priesting (in 1887). To provide a genuinely English, rather than Austrian or Romano-Russian flavour, there was also a major relic of St Thomas of Canterbury, housed in a silver bust (now kept at the successor establishment to Storrington at Muston, near Filey in Yorkshire).[18]

Judging by the way it drew the literary-minded, Storrington was clearly a special spot.[19] Hilaire Belloc (1870–1953) was attracted to the place, which lay less than ten miles from the house — King's Land, outside the Sussex hamlet of Shipley — he had made his life-long home in 1906.[20] He was inspired by his contact with the canons, and more specifically with the artworks in what he termed their 'Hall', to write his ballade-like poem *Courtesy*. He sent the Prior of Storrington the poem in his own hand, signed and dated accordingly. The poem is dated 17 May 1908, a time of year when, weather permitting, the glories of the English countryside would attract walkers far less hardened than Belloc. It celebrates the 'courtesy' involved in a series of painterly images of the Annunciation (Filippino Lippi, 1406–69), the Visitation (Mariotto Albertinelli, 1474–1515), and the Epiphany (Sandro Botticelli, c. 1445–1510),[21]

15 *Monastère de Storrington, Ordre de Prémontré, Fondateur M. le Duc de Norfolk* (Paris: no publisher, 1884). Frigolet Archives, Cartons Storrington, E28. Benefactors acquired a booklet-sized document entitled 'A nos bienfaiteurs de France, d'Angleterre, et de l'Autriche-Hongrie, les prospects de Frigolet reconnaissants, 1884'. Frigolet Archives, Cartons Storrington, E28.

16 Gillett, *Shrine of Our Lady of England at Storrington*, p. 4.

17 *Storrington 1882–1982*, p. 7. Muston Archives.

18 Ian McClean, O.Praem., 'Le Prieuré de Notre Dame d'Angleterre', in Daudet, Plouvier and Souchon, *Les Prémontrés au XIXe siècle*, pp. 239–43.

19 For the setting, see Joan Ham, *Victorian and Edwardian Storrington* (Chichester: Phillimore, 1983).

20 A. N. Wilson, *Hilaire Belloc. A Biography* (London: Hamish Hamilton, 1984), p. 117. Wilson, not a pious man, does not, among Belloc's works, select *Courtesy* for particular comment.

21 Now held at Muston, the first and third are Medici Society prints, the second print, which has weathered time best, is of Flemish or Dutch provenance.

but there is also a suggestion that the act of the 'monks' in inviting Belloc to step inside shares the same divine quality. Belloc did not forget the White Canons, sending them in 1953 a signed copy of a first edition, as it were: the text of the first print version in the *Dublin Review*, now in the possession of St Mary's Priory, Muston.

Other notables settled in or near the village. Wilfrid Meynell (1852–1948), converted by the influence of the Dominican tertiary Hilary Pepler (1878–1951), was editor of two 'niche' Catholic journals: *The Weekly Register*—a job he undertook at the request of Cardinal Henry Edward Manning (1808–92), the second archbishop of Westminster (the paper was a popular rival to the *Tablet*). and *Merry England*, a neo-mediaeval enterprise, with a surprisingly wide range of contributors, and his own initiative and property. Meynell lived at 'Humphrey's Homestead', between Storrington and Greatham, with his wife Alice (1847–1922), regarded as a candidate for the post of poet laureate after the death of Lord Tennyson's (1809–92) rather underwhelming successor Alfred Austin (1835–1913). Robert Bridges (1844–1930) was the (perfectly worthy) successful contender, but her failure to be chosen was, at least in part, misogynist. As the London *Times* commented, 'Feminists would add, and not without some reason, that there is Mrs Meynell; perhaps to make her Laureate would help to satisfy those eminent persons who wish to admit more women to the Civil Service'.[22]

The Meynells were responsible for bringing to Storrington—and specifically to the priory—the Preston born and Ushaw College educated poet Francis Thompson (1859–1907). A victim of opium addiction, Thompson had been living rough on the streets of Charing Cross, but in 1888 submission of his poem *The Passion of Mary* for possible inclusion in *Merry England* led to the discovery of his genius.[23] In the words of his most recent biographer, 'Amid his enforced abstinence [at the Storrington of the canons] and despite the constant agony of his withdrawal symptoms, suddenly poetry began to spill out of him in a remorseless torrent', a phrase which may unconsciously reflect the weight of Thompson's diction, often of stunning beauty yet overloaded by his own linguistic inventions.[24] Since most of the Storrington canons were French, a barrier of language and culture limited the sympathy

---

22 *The Times* for 6 June, 1913, cited in June Badeni, *The Slender Tree. A Life of Alice Meynell* (Padstow: Tabb House, 1981), p. 219. For Thompson's relation with Mrs Meynell, 'my own dear lady and mother', see *ibid.*, pp. 73–4, 77–82, 107–12, 114.

23 For an account of the delicate diplomacy whereby the Meynells took him from the gutter see Brigid M. Boardman, *Between Heaven and Charing Cross. The Life of Francis Thompson* (New Haven, CT: Yale University Press, 1988), pp. 94–9, 104–7.

24 Kenneth Shenton, *O My Hornby and My Barlow Long Ago. The Life of the Poet Francis Thompson, 1859–1907* (Nantwich: Max Books, 2019), pp. 47–8.

they could provide. Yet the even tenor, and quality, of their liturgical life was restorative—not least of his imaginative life as a poet. 'The rhythm and regularity of the daily recitation of the Divine Office revived the meaning the liturgy had for him as he had been introduced to it in his Ushaw days. Now it went far deeper in the reassurance of its recurring pattern woven from divine, natural and human life.'[25] Lodging in the priory from 1889 to 1890, he wrote within its walls poems as different as the lengthy *Ode to the Setting Sun*, a tremendous celebration of the rhythms of the cosmos, Christocentric yet indebted to ancient Greece,[26] and the brief and simple lyric *Daisy*, named for a child from Storrington village and characteristic of the other pole of his complex literary persona.[27]

It was at the priory that he began writing what is by far his best known poem, *The Hound of Heaven*, since translated into over sixty languages, and appealing to readers well beyond the limits of the visible Church. The divine hound pursues a prey that twists and turns in its attempts to find a substitute for God.[28] The poem is filled with literary echoes. Thompson had a capacious memory, which was just as well: he had complained to Wilfrid Meynell about the priory's shortage of books.[29] Libraries, alas, are not always a Premonstratensian priority. (The plan of the last ruling abbot of Prémontré, Jean-Baptiste L'Écuy, 1740–1834, for an ambitious library scheme, intended as a model for the Order at large, was scuppered by the Revolution.[30])

The Modernist theologian and former Jesuit George Tyrrell (1861–1909) came to live in Storrington village in 1907, his patron Maude Petre (1863–1942) improvising a study for him from a hay-store and garden room in the grounds of Mulberry House in the High Street.[31] Tyrrell had been dismissed from the Society in February 1906. When efforts to have his position regularized (not as a Jesuit but as a secular priest)

---

25 Boardman, *Between Heaven and Charing Cross*, p. 109.

26 *Ibid.*, pp. 115–27.

27 *Ibid.*, pp. 129–30.

28 *Ibid.*, pp. 135–42. For the text of the poems, see Brigid M. Boardman (ed.), *The Poems of Francis Thompson. A New Edition* (London and New York: Continuum, 2001).

29 John Evangelist Walsh (ed.), *The Letters of Francis Thompson* (New York: Hawthorn Books, 1969), pp. 25–6.

30 Ardura, *Premostratensi*, pp. 286–8; for a fuller account of this impressive figure, see Berthe Ravary, *Prémontré dans la tourmente révolutionnaire. La vie de Jean-Baptiste L'Ecuy, dernier abbé général des Prémontrés en France, 1740–1834* (Paris: Grasset, 1955).

31 There is a fine modern biography of Tyrrell: Nicholas Sagovsky, *On God's Side. A Life of George Tyrrell* (Oxford: Clarendon Press, 1990); for Petre, see Clyde F. Crews, *English Catholic Modernism. Maude Petre's Way of Faith* (Notre Dame, IN: University of Notre Dame Press, 1984).

came to nothing, he was attracted to Storrington village as a quiet place where, according to Petre, he could count on not only the presence of a cousin and the cousin's family, but the friendship of the canons as well. His daily round became a mixture of sacred and profane. 'When he came into regular residence at Storrington in May, 1907, he slept at the Monastery and spent the day in his room at Mulberry House.'[32] Though impeded from celebrating Mass he was not, for all that, an excommunicate. 'He was glad, as he told me, to be near the church, where he communicated every morning at 6. 30, and which he often visited during the day. Then, too, the Prior [Xavier de Fourvière Rieux, 1853–1912[33]] and he were the best of friends, and he [Tyrrell] was a source of life and encouragement to men [the Premonstratensians] somewhat pressed by material necessities, who led a fairly monotonous life with few Catholic neighbours.'[34] Petre describes how Tyrrell involved himself in the Frigolet canons' studies of English and a hymnal on which they were working where some of the translations—whether from Latin or French she does not say—were his own. 'Altogether, his relations with the community, while based on no intellectual sympathy, seemed to promise a permanence of mutual goodwill.'[35]

In May 1906 Tyrrell wrote to his friend Abbé Henri Bremond (1865–1933), historian of early modern French spirituality and himself both a former Jesuit and a Modernist sympathizer, describing the priory in original terms:

> These 3 jolly Devil-may-care anti-Jesuit monks of Aix are most anxious to fill their empty priory with paying guests and offer me two good rooms and everything else for 30/– a week. I put all possible ecclesiastical difficulties before the Prior but he only pished and pshawed, and say [sic] he would entertain the Devil if he chose and no bishop should say him nay. He says I can have all my lady friends to dine and visit me as much as I like—the *one* restriction is that "pour les misérables convéniences" they must not sleep in the priory. Yesterday he had Hattie [Urquhart, a relative of his cousin William by marriage], Mrs Tyrrell [wife of his cousin, who lived in Storrington] and Miss Ormsby [unidentified] at lunch; the 2 former have been having meals there for 3 weeks. The food and wine is Provençal. He is longing for you to come over. It is very queer; very medieval. In a sense they are pagan; and yet very truly, because unconsciously, Christian

---

32 Maude Petre, *Autobiography and Life of George Tyrrell* (London: Edward Arnold, 1912), II., p. 315.

33 On this figure, see Ardura, *L'Abbaye Saint-Michel de Frigolet*, pp. 271–7.

34 Petre, *Autobiography and Life of George Tyrrell*, II., p. 315.

35 *Ibid.*

and human.[36]

In June 1907 Tyrrell addressed himself in writing to the Prior in more autobiographical mode. 'It seems plain that Storrington must be my centre—the *terminus ex quo* and *ad quem* of my wanderings'. It was not entirely 'convenable' (Tyrrell uses the French word in the middle of an English letter) to sleep or breakfast at Mulberry House, the home of a single woman. After these preliminaries he came quickly to the topic of his ecclesiastical situation. Though Pope Pius was 'bitterly hostile', he for his part had 'very many friends among the Cardinals who utterly condemn the action of the Pope in my regard'. If things go well he would recover his celebret and resume Eucharistic celebration. Meanwhile, 'I am too old to enter another Order or to learn a new method; but I would like not to feel quite isolated and St Norbert was the first to open his arms to me'.[37] Xavier de Fourvière Rieux approved of Tyrrell's attempts to normalize his position in the Catholic Church and its priesthood. By way of return Tyrrell sought to do something for the canons of Storrington, the outstanding feature of whose life, in the eye of the observer, was involuntary poverty. In August 1907 he wrote again to the Prior of Storrington, this time with an idea. 'I see the [Premonstratensian] Abbot of Teplá's portrait is in all the illustrated papers of today. He looks very fat and rich and prosperous. I think he might have done something for Storrington if—as the papers say—he is "one of the richest ecclesiastics in the world".'[38] This was no journalistic exaggeration. The Czech abbey of Teplá, then in Austria-Hungary, owned not only thousands of hectares of land, and some factories; it also held a monopoly over the thermal sources at Marienbad, a spa-town favoured by royalty where Edward VII had taken the waters—doubtless the occasion for the epiphany of the 'Prince Abbot' in the British picture-press.[39] It was a kind thought on Tyrrell's part at a time when his own turbulent affairs were drawing to their predestined end.

The moment was scarcely propitious for a happy outcome to his case. *Lamentabili*, a 'Syllabus'—Tyrrell's term—of Modernist texts deemed

36 Letter of 15 May 1906 from George Tyrrell to Henri Bremond, cited in Sagovsky, *On God's Side*, p. 207.

37 Letter of 1 June 1907 from George Tyrrell to Xavier de Fourvière Rieux. Frigolet Archives, Cartons Prêtres, JII 66. The date has been added, with the cautionary note 'probably' by another hand.

38 Letter of 30 August 1907 from George Tyrrell to the Prior of Storrington. Frigolet Archives, Cartons Prêtres, JII 66. The 'Prince Abbot' was Gilbert Helmer (1864–1944).

39 For a contemporary account of the wealth of Teplá (dating from 1914), see Dom Amand Ménager, 'Notes sur les Monastères de Bohème et d'Autriche', in *Lettre aux Amis de Solesmes* 46. 185 (2021), pp. 7–31 (for Teplá, pp. 12–16).

erroneous, had been promulgated by the Holy Office in July 1907, and the systematical anti-Modernist encyclical *Pascendi*, with its devastating clarity, in September of the same year. Friends sympathetic to Tyrrell's thought regretted a letter he now wrote for the authorities, promising not to publish again without permission. This, they felt, would be interpreted at Rome as an act of penitence for his previous opinions. In a last minute telegram to Petre Tyrrell sought to prevent the Storrington canons from dispatching it, but in those far-off days of multiple daily postal collections and deliveries it had already gone by the first post.[40] When he realized that newspaper accounts bore out the premonitions, his 'patience snapped ... Immediately he wrote to the papers disclaiming "submission", and to [Cardinal Domenico] Ferrata [Prefect of the Sacred Congregation of Bishops and Regulars, 1847–1914] retracting his undertaking'.[41]

His subsequent critiques of *Pascendi* in the London *Times* and the Roman *Giornale d'Italia* prompted Peter Amigo (1864–1949), the sixth bishop of Southwark, to forbid him the sacraments—thus inflicting the so-called 'minor excommunication', whereupon, following the wishes of the Prior, he 'withdrew himself and his effects from the Monastery at Storrington, and only attended the church on Sunday for Mass'.[42]

In the autumn of 1907 Xavier de Fourvière Rieux sent a reasoned account of his own actions in the 'Tyrrell Affair' to the editor of the French Catholic paper *La Croix*. He owed it (he told the editor) to his confreres and indeed to himself to furnish a public justification of his role.[43] He wished to put it on record that Tyrrell had 'never raised any doctrinal question' when staying with the canons. His behaviour was 'reserved', 'pious', 'regular'—by which Prior Rieux referred to the former Jesuit's attendance at the liturgical Offices.[44] It was because so many people had urged him to commend Tyrrell to the Roman authorities—not only friends and relations but also 'pious persons' who had noted his 'very pacific spirit' and 'exquisite charity'—that he had felt obliged to intervene with Cardinal Ferrata on Tyrrell's behalf.[45] He wished now to share his 'own impressions [of] the excellent dispositions with which Father Tyrrell seemed to me to be filled'.[46]

---

40 Petre, *Autobiography and Life of George Tyrrell*, II, p. 325.
41 Sagovsky, *On God's Side*, p. 219.
42 Petre, *Autobiography and Life of George Tyrrell*, II, p. 346.
43 Xavier de Fourviere, *L'Affaire de Tyrrell* (Letter of 4 October 1907 to 'Monsieur le Directeur de *La Croix*'). Frigolet Archives, Cartons Prêtres, JII 66.
44 *Ibid.*, p. 2.
45 *Ibid.*, pp. 7–8.
46 *Ibid.*, p. 8.

His initiative had brought results. Ferrata had signed, on 23 August 1907, the crucial letter giving notice that Tyrrell might resume the celebration of Mass, on condition that he refrained from communicating further his theological opinions. But (as subsequent events showed) Tyrrell found intolerable any notion that his silence be construed as theological 'submission' — as it speedily was by certain gentlemen of the Press, both English and Italian. Prior Rieux described his 'desolation' at reading Tyrrell's counterblasts which seemed to come from 'a Protestant pen'.[47] He concluded that Tyrrell had never really entertained a 'just notion of the magisterium of the Church'.[48] That was a 'lacuna' or, better, a 'shadow' that led astray his 'fine intelligence'. He could only assume — bearing in mind Tyrrell's own denominational origins in the Church of Ireland — that the 'old Protestant leaven' had re-activated.[49] Prior Rieux concluded with a passionate appeal to Tyrrell to put into practice the words of the Prodigal Son in St Luke's Gospel, 'I will arise and go to my father' — in this case, Pius X, shepherd of the sheep and lambs, and doctor or teacher whose mission it was to confirm his brethren.[50]

It need hardly be said that the appeal fell on deaf ears, while its uncompromising papalist tone is unlikely to have commended itself to the guardian of the flame, Miss Petre, descendant of a leading English Cisalpine of the Emancipation era. In Tyrrell's final illness, which can be dated from 6 to 15 July 1909, it was she who cared for him at Mulberry House where on 12 July, in a state of semi-consciousness, he received the last Anointing from the hands of the Prior of Storrington, his critical supporter.

> Thinking he might now be very near the end, and that [Charles] Dessoulavey [a Southwark priest befriended by Tyrrell] might not arrive in time, Maude Petre reluctantly sent for the Prior, calling him away from high mass. While she held Tyrrell's head, the Prior recited several acts of faith and exhorted him to submit himself totally to the teaching of the Church. It is possible that Tyrrell could hear, but he did not respond. The Prior concluded by giving him extreme unction, but not Communion, as he probably could not swallow. After that he fell into a peaceful sleep.[51]

On 14 July Bremond gave Tyrrell, still only partially conscious, sacramental absolution and was present the following day when he died.[52]

---

47 *Ibid.*, p. 13.
48 *Ibid.*, p. 15.
49 *Ibid.*
50 *Ibid.*, p. 18.
51 Nicholas Sagovsky, *On God's Side*, p. 260.
52 Petre, *Autobiography and Life of George Tyrrell*, II, pp. 420–3.

On 17 July Bishop Amigo intimated that unless Tyrrell had made an actual retractation on his deathbed he could not be buried with Catholic rites. He was interred instead in Storrington's Anglican churchyard, at a ceremony during which Bremond, not wearing vestments, spoke, and recited not the Catholic burial rite but a set of simple prayers (the Our Father, a Kyrie, and the psalm *De profundis*).[53] The glebe of the historic parish church adjoins priory land, so this ceremony would probably have been visible from the Frigolet canons' upper stories.

'Three days later', so Petre tersely records, 'the Bishop of Southwark wired to the Prior of Storrington: "Do not allow Bremond to say Mass".'[54] Petre would herself be buried near Tyrrell, though since her excommunication was only local (that is, restricted to the Southwark diocese) she merited a Requiem Mass north of the Thames, at the Convent of the Assumption, Kensington Square.[55]

A far less dramatic figure equally integral to Catholic Storrington in the following generation was the historian and hagiographer Donald Attwater (1892–1977) who lived in West Street. St Norbert is not omitted in his revision, and condensations in 'Dictionary' form, of the classic *Lives of the Saints* by Alban Butler (1710–73), president of the English seminary at Saint-Omer.[56]

The interest of these literary and theological connexions of the priory must not detract attention from the early life of the community itself. At the beginnings of Norbertine Storrington, five men were dispatched by the Provençal abbey in 1882. Owing to shortage of funds no building work on the planned priory-cum-church began till 1887. Yet by some point in the later 1880s the numbers in community had risen to fourteen.[57] They included the first English recruits, Bede Rothwell and Osmund Kirke. Both were Mancunians and received the habit in 1888. Rothwell had already been priested, for the Congregation of the Passion, an eighteenth-century Italian institute that had played a significant part in the early Catholic Revival in England. Kirke, a convert,

53 Sagovsky, *On God's Side*, p. 261

54 Petre, *Autobiography and Life of George Tyrrell*, II, p. 447.

55 James T. Kelly (ed.), *The Letters of Baron Friedrich von Hügel and Maude D. Petre* (Leuven: Peeters, 2003), p. xxxiii.

56 Catherine Rachel John, 'Donald Attwater, 1892–1977: A Man for His Time and Ours', *Chesterton Review* 29/4 (2003), pp. 519–27. Norbert receives a four-page treatment, considerably more than the median length of entries, in the third volume of Attwater's 1956 re-working of Alban Butler's *Lives of the Saints*, a text condensed in his pocket *Dictionary of the Saints*, originally (in 1936/1948) an index to the Butler *Lives*, and subsequently re-issued in various formats and editions before further revision by his daughter and memorialist Catherine Rachel John in 1983/1995.

57 McClean, 'Le Prieuré de Notre Dame d'Angleterre', pp. 240–1.

became a 'frère convers' rather than a 'frère de choeur', though he was deemed educationally fit for Ordination.[58] An indispensable figure was Louis de Gonzague Daras, the first prior and a willing workhorse, who sought funds for the new enterprise all over central Europe as well as in France itself.

Finance was never easy. At first the little community tried to make a living from winemaking; this was climatically premature. Efforts were diverted instead to chocolate-manufacture and printing. When the canons got into debt with builders Eugénie made a contribution, though some idea of the trials of an empress of the French in England is glimpsed when we read that the builder would not accept her French banknotes, on the ground that the previous consignment of francs had been dirty, greasy, and stank of garlic and fish. She paid him in gold instead.[59]

A good start for publications directed to the English-speaking public was made by the first issues of a modest journal entitled *Prémontré Annals. History — Archaeology — Literature*. This described itself as 'a quarterly journal published under the direction of the Reverend Father Louis de Gonzague, prior of the Premonstratensians at Storrington, Sussex'. Expressing interest in the pre-Reformation sites, cartularies, and any other physical remains of mediaeval British predecessors, the concept behind *Prémontré Annals* was ambitious, not least as regards distribution: outlets were named in London, Edinburgh, Dublin, Paris, Brussels, Vienna, Budapest, and Rome as well as, obviously, Storrington itself.[60] In the years after the Second World War when Storrington passed into the hands of Tongerlo, its bulletins (*Norbertines* and *White Canons*) would be much more modest.

The early days were not without their problems, quite irrespective of financial hurdles. In an undated letter, Abbot Boniface scolded Louis de Gonzague Daras in no uncertain terms. 'Your absences have been a great inconvenience for the community at Storrington, and when you were present your internal administration was deplorable.'[61] The absences

58 Ardura, *L'Abbaye Saint-Michel de Frigolet*, pp. 297–300. Disappointingly, both died young — at any rate by present-day standards, in their 40s and 50s respectively.

59 Edith Wick, 'Early Days of the Premonstratensian Order in Sussex', *Sussex County Magazine*, December 1941. Muston Archives.

60 From the cover of the second issue of the first year of *Prémontré Annals*, 1882. Muston Archives. In 1881, the Frigolet mouthpiece entitled, evidently in a spirit of Marian devotion, *Cour d'honneur de Marie* had adopted as sub-title the rather more sober name of *Annales Norbertines*, Ardura, *L'Abbaye Saint-Michel de Frigolet*, p. 44. Ardura notes that the devotional title was somewhat misleading: the review was militant, at daggers drawn with anti-clerical Republicanism, p. 63.

61 Undated letter from Abbot Paulin Boniface to the Prior of Storrington. Frigolet

were not all a matter of essential fund-raising. As correspondence with the third Marquess of Bute explored in Chapter 8 will show, Daras had become a much-travelled expert on mediaeval English Premonstratensian sites as well as an avid reader in the library of the British Museum.[62]

Moreover, not all the locals were as philo-Catholic as Daras had fondly believed. The local Anglican rector forbade his parishioners to attend the canons' services and when his servant boy disobeyed the injunction lost no time in giving him the sack.[63] There were patriotic anti-Catholic protests, which, unlike at Crowle, were more than verbal in character. In 1887, a pamphlet produced by the canons under the title 'An Event of the Jubilee Year' (the jubilee in question was Victoria's), had as its centre-piece a 'manly protest against outrages' on the part of 'A Sussex Man'. The letter to the *Catholic Times*, from one who described himself as 'born and bred a Protestant of the Church of England', deplored an arson attack on the priory, only two or three years after the vandalizing of a rather large and public crucifix in the grounds. The letter had originally been sent to the *West Sussex Gazette* whose editor (or proprietor) had not thought fit to publish.[64]

There could also be outrage (and protest) of a different kind. In 1895 a canon was accused of impropriety with a Religious Sister, and there was a suggestion that his was not the only case. John Baptist Butt (1826–99), the fourth bishop of Southwark, was up in arms.[65] At first he wanted to close down the house entirely. But he had second thoughts. (He should have had plenty of material to ponder: the Congregation of Propaganda Fide ordered three consecutive canonical visitations.[66]) The following year, on the eve of his retirement, Butt asked instead for more canons to be sent.[67]

Archives, Cartons Storrington, E29. Daras was in office from 1882 to 1888.

62 The Frigolet Archives contain a vast number of the results of his research and other writing, which occupy twenty-nine boxes of documents: Cartons Pretres, JII, 23.1 to 23, 30, with the exception of one box devoted to his correspondence, JII 23, 29.

63 Unsigned Memoir entitled 'Storrington 1882–1982', p. 7. Muston Archives.

64 *An Event of the Jubilee Year*. Muston Archives.

65 There may have been an inter-generational memory of the short-lived (Third Order) Convent of Norbertine Sisters at Sutton, Surrey (transferred thence from an initial start at Spalding), which his predecessor, Robert Aston Coffin, C.Ss.R. (1819–85), third bishop of Southwark, had been obliged to close owing to scandal in the summer of 1882, releasing the Sisters from their vows. This, however, was a Tongerlo, not a Frigolet, initiative.

66 Ardura, *L'Abbaye de Saint-Michel de Frigolet*, p. 76.

67 On the early history of Storrington (and Farnborough), see Bernard Ardura, 'Introduction', in Xavier de Fourvière [Albert Rieux], *Escourregudo en Anglo-Terro (Promenade en Angleterre). L'Angleterre du XIXe siècle vue par un Provençal* (Marseille, Editions Jeanne Laffitte, 2005), pp. 5–27. This book, in Provençal with a French trans-

That crisis surmounted, the project seemed to thrive. An important marker in time had been the priorial appointment in 1903 of Tyrrell's friend Xavier de Fourvière Rieux, a literary figure of some standing in the modern revival of the Provençal language and its literature.[68] Rieux had an acute mind, and, unlike Daras, he was an effective administrator. But even before his arrival development was in hand. In 1893 a small school had opened, with the Duke of Norfolk's help, for local Catholic families ('small' was clearly thought to be beautiful, there were never more than between fifteen and twenty pupils). That was on adjacent Kithurst Hill, the highest point for the countryside around.[69] The foundation stone for the church and priory themselves had been laid in 1902, the year before Xavier de Fourvière Rieux's priorship began. His predecessor, Barthélémy Guigue, prior between 1900 and 1903, had taken the decision to erect a fully equipped conventual church.[70] Unlike the minor basilica in Manchester, its small scale meant it could never have become, however, the *abbatiale* of a great convent.

Stone-laying is, by definition, only a start. In 1904, a temporary chapel, precedent to the present priory-and-parish church, was blessed in hope of better things to come. A farm building, separated from the east side of the cloister by a sizeable vegetable garden, served as a printing works for priory publications.[71] The priory church would not be completed until 1919, and the priory itself, constructed on a traditional cloister plan, with the church (built on a north-south axis) as its western side, was left unfinished until 1930.

lation, concerns two journeys through England (and in one case Scotland) made by the author, from 20 June to 21 August and 19 September to 21 November 1895.

68 In addition to his published writings, exclusively in Provençal, the Frigolet Archives contain a large number of texts in both French and Provençal, ranging from poetry to history, as well as homiletic and retreat material, Cartons Prêtres, JII 71, 3 to 71. 18.

69 The school survived the Frigolet canons themselves, not closing its doors till 1950, after which it became, successively, offices for the Norbertine-founded charity Aid to the Church in Need, a boxing club for boys of the parish, and a 'grace and favour' dwelling place for the farm workers on priory land. The building, Gerston Lodge, is now a private dwelling with the name Norbert House. Information provided by Martin Gosling, O.Praem., in a conversation of 13 June 2023.

70 *Pièces justicatives* for this claim can be found in Frigolet Archives, Cartons Prêtres, JII 70.

71 Subsequently, in the 1960s, it became diocesan offices for the new Catholic diocese of Arundel and Brighton. It is now leased by the French 'new ecclesial movement' Chemin Neuf. Information provided by Martin Gosling, O.Praem., in a conversation of 13 June 2023. At the time of writing, Chemin Neuf used the property to house refugees from the Russo-Ukrainian war, as I discovered on my visit of 22 June 2023.

Though construction proceeded by fits and starts (Norbertine economics at Frigolet left no other option) the whole ensemble was undeniably attractive. Despite its preponderance of brick rather than stone, the little monastery, with its modest proportions, was well-suited to its natural and human environment on the South Downs. It looked as if Frigolet had made a good beginning.

~ 7 ~

Thrown on Life's Surge:
A Scattering of English Missions

S TORRINGTON SOON HAD EXALTED CONNEXIONS in the shape of its own seeding at Farnborough, in the neighbouring county of Hampshire, where the canons were called upon to serve the 'imperial mausoleum' of the Napoleonic dynasty in its Second Empire incarnation. In 1888 the bodies of Napoleon III (1808–73), who had died in English exile in 1873, and his ill-fated son, the Prince Imperial ('Napoleon IV', 1856–79), who fell victim to Zulu assegais when in the service of the British in South Africa, would be buried in a bespoke crypt whose generous dimensions reflected the station of the occupants in life.

The widowed and now childless Eugénie had bought from the publisher Thomas Longman (1804–79) the house called 'Farnborough Hill', described by one historian of the Second Empire as 'in some respects a virtual court in exile'.[1] She now acquired nearby 'Coombe Hill' on which to build the future monastery and its church. Her aim was straightforward. Like the historic kings of France in the *Basilique royale de Saint-Denis*, her husband and son were to have a perpetual guarantee of Masses and other prayers, courtesy of a resident monastic community supplied with this commission. In November 1886 the 'Chronique' section of the Frigolet publication *Cour d'honneur de Marie* reported that the Empress had paid the Provençal abbey the signal compliment of inviting its canons to serve her new foundation.[2] By 1889 the buildings

---

1 W. H. C. Smith, *The Empress Eugénie and Farnborough* (Winchester: Hampshire County Council, 2001), p. 8. See also Dorothy A. Mostyn, *The Story of a House. The History of Farnborough Hill* (Farnborough: St Michael's Abbey Press, 1999 [1980]). The purchase of the house by the adjoining convent school in 1927 led to the dismantling of the interiors and the dispersal of Eugenie's carefully assembled art collection, a monument to the Second Empire achievement which has been lovingly recreated in images and prose in Anthony Geraghty, *The Empress Eugénie in England. Art, Architecture, Collecting* (Chicago, IL: University of Chicago Press, 2022).

2 'Chronique', *Cour d'honneur de Marie* 23/275 (1886), p. 262.

were finished, in the Flamboyant Gothic style rarely seen in England; the architect was (naturally) a Frenchman: Gabriel-Hippolyte Destailleur (1822–93). Destailleur served her well, creating 'a small masterpiece of ecclesiastical architecture in which all the inspiration is French with clever borrowings from the vernacular of that country's different regions'.[3] Only the choir-stalls and mural decoration had to be added, which they were by 1891.[4]

Dom Placid Higham, monk of Farnborough, writing in 1959 in the Prinknash journal *Pax*, reported how 'The annals of this first chapter in the history of our house are briefly recorded in a neat French hand and fill a slender volume, recently lent to us through the kindness of the Very Reverend Father Prior of Storrington'.[5] On 31 August 1887 four Religious from that priory, along with a junior from Frigolet itself,[6] arrived at Farnborough under the leadership of Ambroise Garreau (1827–94), who had earlier served as the Procurator of the Primitive Observance canons of Prémontré in Rome. The Empress clearly made some considerable effort to please these new chaplains. Until their church was ready she allowed them to worship in her private chapel at Farnborough Hill. She gave them a rich haul of vestments, suited to the Premonstratensian taste for the ceremonially sumptuous, but not, to their disappointment, relics which, apparently, she disliked. She furnished the conventual buildings with imperial mementoes from Napoleon III's summer residence in Biarritz, his favourite watering place, and from his last residence, Chislehurst's Camden Place, items which may (or may not) have been to their taste. Their duties were also laid out: the recitation of the Divine Office, whether in church or crypt, the celebration of Sunday Mass, and the 'anniversary Masses' of 9 January, 5 May, and 1 June (death-dates of Napoleon III, Napoleon I, and the Prince Imperial respectively), together with thrice-weekly Low Masses for the intentions of the Empress.[7]

---

3 Smith, *The Empress Eugénie and Farnborough*, p. 7.

4 For a description of church and crypt, see [Monks of St Michael's Abbey], *St Michael's Abbey, Farnborough* (Andover: Pitkin Unichrome, 1998), the historical section of which has airbrushed out all reference to the original Norbertine custodians, unlike the earlier brochure by Placid Higham, OSB, *St Michael's Benedictine Abbey. A History and Guide* (Farnborough: Community of St Michael's Abbey, no date), pp. 13–14.

5 Placid Higham, OSB, 'The Early Annals of St Michael's Farnborough', *Pax* 49/290 (Summer 1959), pp. 44–50, and here at p. 44.

6 Higham speaks of a 'layman', but a writer with access to the 'cartons' in the Frigolet Archives is likely to be the better guide: thus Ardura, *L'Abbaye Saint-Michel de Frigolet*, p. 62.

7 W. H. C. Smith, 'Les Prémontrés et l'impératrice Eugénie á Farnborough en

On 29 October 1887 John Vertue (1826–1900), the first bishop of Portsmouth, paid an official visit, registering his pleasure at having the Premonstratensians of the Congregation of France in his diocese, and expressing the hope that they would be of assistance in the parochial life of the local church.[8] This was not at all the Empress's plan, and raised an issue which would cause difficulties in the future. But the die was cast. On 9 January 1888 the bodies of the emperor and his son were conveyed from Chislehurst to Farnborough in a special train and met on arrival by two regiments of Royal Artillery (at Queen Victoria's orders). At the door of the new priory church Abbot Boniface received the coffins liturgically, assisted by Prior Ambroise Garreau, and after the singing of the Office of the Dead they were interred in the sarcophagi prepared for them.[9]

In Higham's report on the early Farnborough annals, Prior Garreau soon gave way to a successor, indicated only by the characteristically Norbertine monastic name of Evermode,[10] who two years later was himself replaced by Joseph Ibos (born 1852),[11] the last Norbertine superior. The latter continued in office until the departure of the Premonstratensians in 1895. By that date Farnborough had a community of eight, leaving free only a single choirstall in the church. As Higham noted, it would

1887', in Dauzet, Plouvier and Souchon, *Les Prémontrés au XIXe siècle*, pp. 230–7, and here at p. 234.

8 *Ibid.*

9 *Ibid.*, pp. 234–5.

10 No 'Evermode' occurs, however, in the listing of Frigolet canons at Farnborough in the *Catholic Directories* for Great Britain in the relevant years. Bernard Ardura, in the history of Frigolet detailed above, appears to have no knowledge of an intervening priorship between those of Garreau and Ibos. But a letter from Abbot Boniface strongly suggests an Evermode, who was obliged to resign as superior and subsequently sought dispensation from his vows: Letter of 12 May 1890 from Abbot Paulin Boniface to Prior Joseph Ibos. Frigolet Archives, Cartons Storrington, E29. A letter of 26 November 1895, written from the fashionable Parisian parish of Notre Dame des Victoires, addressed to Denis Bonnefoy, O.Praem., and signed 'Evermode', implies that the letter-writer had not only an inside knowledge of the collapse of Norbertine expectations at Farnborough but a crucial role in events. It was 'in the hope that before taking so grave a decision the Empress would temporize in order to find a means of conciliation' that 'I wrote to her Majesty, on the occasion of her feast, a letter in which I pleaded the cause of the Premonstratensians with the heart of a brother'. Frigolet Archives, Cartons Prêtres, JII 30.2. Incidentally, the letter's closing promise of prayers to Our Lady of Victories 'for compensations and consolations for our venerable archbishop of Aix and for you' points to a context in the fall from canonical grace of Abbot Boniface.

11 Owing to Ibos leaving the Congregation in 1895, his death date is not recorded in the Frigolet Necrology: see Ardura, *L'Abbaye Saint-Michel de Frigolet*, p. 76, footnote 12.

never be filled — not, that is, by a Premonstratensian. For the priory would pass into the hands of the Solesmes Benedictines in 1895, and subsequently, with the arrival of monks of Prinknash abbey in Gloucestershire, to the Subiaco Congregation of the Benedictine Order in 1947. This change entailed a significant degree of pastoral retrenchment. Bishop Vertue had made Farnborough a parish church in all but name, a quasi-parochial charge subsequently refused by the monks of Solesmes. For Farnborough's townspeople, St Norbert's, consisting of a chapel and attached school, had been founded elsewhere, on a site in Peabody Lane. But this too offended the contemplative proclivities of the French Congregation monks and had to be offloaded onto Salesians in 1898. The Norbertine annals seen by Placid Higham could record other missionary activities of the Fathers in the surrounding villages — copying, presumably unwittingly, the pattern of development of the Tongerlo canons in Crowle and Spalding.

To Norbertine Farnborough Bishop Vertue further attached some sort of spiritual jurisdiction over the district of Bracknell in the contiguous country of Berkshire. Bracknell was not yet the 'New Town' it later became, nor was its name as yet a household word as would shortly be the case with the invention of the unforgettable character of Lady Bracknell in Oscar Wilde's (1854–1900) play *The Importance of Being Earnest* (written in 1895). On the closure of the Catholic chapel at nearby Warfield Park (the home of the Benn Walshes, later Barons Ormathwaite), the Reilly family of Kells House in Church Road offered a room to serve as a Mass-centre. In accepting the invitation, Premonstratensians entered the picture in this Berkshire village. By 1894 Joseph Ibos had acquired two acres of land, sufficient for a church and a school. The following year an 'iron church' was erected. It would be the origin of the present parish of St Joseph (in 2008 combined with a later initiative, a parish dedicated to the Elizabethan 'Pearl of York', St Margaret Clitherow [1555–86]).[12]

Dom Higham was intrigued by the question of why exactly the canons regular of the Primitive Observance had left Farnborough (and thus Bracknell). Had they gone of their own free will, or had they been pushed? There was a rumour that the last prior was a fervent Republican and had given offence to the Empress by an untimely comment while preaching in the august presence.[13] *Prima facie*, given Frigolet's history,

12 https://bracknellcatholic church.org/parish-life/history/, consulted 17 April 2023.

13 Nicholas Paxton, 'The Imperial Abbey at Farnborough, 1883–1920', *Recusant History* 28/4 (2007), pp. 575–92, while willing to credit the rumour of the Republicanism of Prior Ibos (on the basis of an anonymous article entitled 'Farnborough' in *White Canons* I [1973], p. 27), remains essentially agnostic about the causality of the 'dismissal'; 'The Imperial Abbey at Farnborough, 1883–1920', p. 580.

that seems a trifle unlikely. The forcible expulsion of the canons by Republican dragoons, in the teeth of opposition from a hostile crowd, had been a *cause célèbre* in France, commemorated in a vast painting, *Siège de Frigolet*, by François Wenzel in 1881.[14] Higham was inclined to think the departure 'connected in some way with the administration of the church', a guess with something to be said for it. The demands of chaplaincraft at an imperial mausoleum were not light. When in January 1888 the remains of the emperor and his son were brought to the priory and re-interred in so 'flamboyant' a setting, the event naturally attracted the attention of an international public.[15] Queen Victoria, for instance, lost no time in paying her respects, coming on 3 March of that year. Despite her notorious dislike of the Church of Rome, she was formally introduced to the canons, and gave it as her verdict that their habit was 'so harmonious in its simplicity', which was gracious enough.[16] Visits by Bonapartist devotees or the simply curious were time-consuming, particularly if they were reigning sovereigns like Luis I of Portugal (1838–89), or Oscar II of Sweden-Norway (1829–1907), who expected punctilious attendance. For her part, the Empress appears to have disapproved of the pastoral activities of the canons outside their enclosure. Doubtless it took them away from mausoleum duties.[17] It may also have been the case that her financial largesse was not excessive.

The simplest explanation, however, did not occur to the Benedictine writer, who perhaps was unaware of events at Frigolet itself. Documents in the archives of the abbey of Solesmes, the motherhouse of the Congregation of France, suggest that the Empress was shocked when news reached her of the effective deposition of Abbot Boniface and its cause—carnal desire compounded, or so it could be argued, with fraud—and thereafter refused to receive in audience canons seeking a reprieve of execution.[18] A letter to Denis Bonnefoy (1853–99) from one of the empress's ladies demonstrates that the administrator of Frigolet sought to save the day—but too late. 'The Empress charges me with

14 The event also inspired published poetry, or at least verse: Jean de la Tour d'Allaine, *Le Siège de Frigolet. Poème épique en trois chants* (Aix: Nicot, 1880).

15 *Farnborough to Storrington, 1887–1895*, photocopied manuscript, Muston Archives.

16 Higham, 'The Early Annals of St Michael's Farnborough', p. 48.

17 Ardura, *L'Abbaye Saint-Michel de Frigolet*, p. 76.

18 Conversation of 1 October 2023 with Fra François-Marie Pourcelet, the archivist of Frigolet. The archivist emeritus of Solesmes wrote to his opposite number in the Provençal abbey, 'Toutes les archives de Farnborough ont été entreposées à Solesmes', e-letter of 22 March 2020 from Dom Louis Soltner to Fra François-Marie Pourcelet. I understand that Fra Pourcelet intends to pursue this matter further at Solesmes itself.

telling you ... that the *démarche*—very praiseworthy, though it is—you are attempting in her regard is rendered useless by the installation of the Benedictine Fathers at the priory.'[19] For his part Higham could only conclude that, despite their precipitate displacement, the Premonstratensians had left behind a good reputation, both for hospitality in the monastery and for pastoral zeal in their work in the neighbourhood.[20]

Storrington and Farnborough are less than forty miles apart, and Farnborough and Bracknell little more than ten. But Frigolet canons looked further afield than these Southern locations for their mission *ad Anglos*. In the English Midlands, they were not asked to begin from scratch, as at Farnborough, but to step into a place already prepared for them. At Weston-in-Arden, in Warwickshire, an extensive property made available to the Frigolet canons in 1888 was the gift of Richard Lerins de Bary (1841–91), the owner of Weston Hall. By the late Victorian period the term 'Arden' had become restricted to (some of) Warwickshire, though the historic Forest of Arden, thickly wooded, and bounded but not crossed by Roman roads, had taken in much of the Midland counties. In Shakespeare's *As You Like It*, the Forest seems to stand for an iconic 'Merry England', possibly connected with the survival of Recusancy among local families.[21] This, however, was not where the de Barys were coming from. The donor's father, Richard Brome de Bary (1813–58), a barrister and landed gentleman, had become a Catholic under Tractarian influence in 1842, the year after his son's birth. A domestic oratory in his house, served by Dominican friars from the Leicestershire town of Hinckley, had functioned as the first Post-Reformation Catholic chapel in the immediate area.[22] When the Dominicans lost their (previously Flanders-based) school and priory at Carshalton, in Surrey, they had made Hinckley their principal base, a centre for not only the re-created

19 Letter of 25 November 1895 from E. d'Allonville to Denis Bonnefoy, O.Praem. Frigolet Archives, Cartons Prêtres, JII 30. 2.

20 For a more negative assessment, see Desmond Seward, *Eugénie. The Empress and her Empire* (Stroud: Sutton, 2004). Accepting the suggestion that the last prior was a Republican, Seward opines that the canons 'seem to have been a boorish and uncouth group', adding for good measure that when the Norbertines finally departed, they left the 'abbey in a state of squalor', p. 267. An essay by W. H. C. Smith ('Four White Canons'), given as source material in Seward's endnotes, which might conceivably provide evidence for these judgements, does not recur, with publishing details, in the bibliography.

21 It should be noted, however, that the Oxford edition of the plays assumes a confusion among critics between Arden and the Ardennes and changes the spelling accordingly. See Jonathan Bate, *Soul of the Age: The Life, Mind and World of William Shakespeare* (London: Viking, 2008), p. 37.

22 *Our Lady of the Sacred Heart, Weston-in-Arden. A Parish History 1849–2004* (Bulkington: no publisher, 2004), pp. 19–20, 22–3.

school but also a series of missions in the Midland District.[23]

In 1862 Richard Lerins de Bary married Mary Pauline Mostyn, product of a well-known Welsh Catholic family, the Mostyns of Talacre in Flintshire. This alliance sealed the catholicity of the family. It also steeled a resolve to make the village a centre of renewed Catholic life. In 1869 a church dedicated to 'Our Lady of the Sacred Heart' was built at the de Barys' expense. This impelled them to seek out a fresh clerical régime: Dominican energies were in any case increasingly concentrated in the growing towns of Hinckley and Leicester. In the 1880s Capuchin friars came, but also went.[24] In consequence, Louis de Gonzague Daras, who had led the Frigolet contingent to Storrington (and will re-appear in this narrative in Galloway), was asked by the de Bary family to take on, in the name of Abbot Boniface, the Weston enterprise.

In February 1888 the 'Anonymous Notes' transcribed in the Muston Archives describe Pauline de Bary as writing several times to the prior of Storrington about the affairs of the mission, for which the first Premonstratensian rector, François d'Assise Laborde (1862–1930), who arrived in 1889, had rather grand ideas. He wanted a proper monastic church and a house of studies to match. At the heart of England, rural yet strategically placed, it is not difficult to see how Arden could have seemed perfectly situated for a permanent Premonstratensian implantation.

Meanwhile William Bernard Ullathorne (1806–89), the first bishop of Birmingham, a giant of Victorian Catholicism, had become involved. He appears to have been impressed by the Provençal abbot who presented himself at St Mary's College, Oscott, a place of note for the Catholic Revival in England.[25] It was the last year of Ullathorne's life: the meeting transpired in the August before his death on 21 March 1889.[26] Reportedly, he rejoiced that the final act of his long administration (he retired in March 1888) was opening the diocese to the canons of Frigolet.[27] If so, this was somewhat surprising. Ullathorne's most recent biographer noted that, whereas he consistently gave enormous support to the work of Religious Sisters, 'he was not always welcoming to religious priests in missions'.[28] But his particular *bêtes noires* were pushy Jesuits and Fran-

23 Richard Finn, *The Dominicans in the British Isles and Beyond: A New History of the English Province of the Friars Preachers* (Cambridge: Cambridge University Press, 2022), pp. 222–3.

24 *Our Lady of the Sacred Heart, Weston-in-Arden*, pp. 25–6.

25 Judith F. Champ, (ed.), *Oscott College, 1838–1988. A Volume of Commemorative Essays* (Sutton Coldfield: Oscott College, 1988).

26 Idem., *William Bernard Ullathorne, 1806–1889. A Different Kind of Monk* (Leominster: Gracewing, 2006), p. 495.

27 'Chronique', *Cour d'honneur de Marie. Annales Norbertines* 24/287 (1887), p, 263.

28 Champ, *Ullathorne*, p. 441.

ciscans whom mendicancy rendered financially unreliable.[29] Canons regular fleeing an anti-Christian government can have held no special fears. As a Churchman who had fought the good fight with the civil authorities, in Australia as well as England, he may have seen in Abbot Boniface, survivor of the Siege of Frigolet, another of his kind.

Ullathorne's successor Edward Ilsley (1838–1926), the second bishop (later first archbishop) of Birmingham, fixed the catchment area of the Weston mission's activities as inclusive of the villages of Bulkington (the postal address of Weston), Wolvey, Withybrook, Shilton, Austen, and Hawkesbury. These places are all situated in George Eliot (1819–80) country, where northern Warwickshire borders Leicestershire.[30] The following year, 1890, Ilsley added Bedworth, less than two miles to the north-east, where a church dedicated to Francis of Assisi (*c.* 1181–1226) had been opened in 1883.[31]

Bedworth enabled the de Bary foundation at Weston to survive by making possible the upkeep of a house of three or four canons,[32] for Abbot Boniface, subsequently criticized for laisser-faire administration, was always clear on one point: he would not consider any pastoral commitment which required a canon regular to live alone. In the 1850s there had been a quartet of Recusant families in Bedworth. Accustomed hitherto to walking either to Coventry or Nuneaton for Mass, they summoned Victorian self-help to their aid. In 1875 local lay initiative fitted out a disused shop as a Mass-house, to be replaced in 1877 — again, through lay action — by a purpose-built chapel, dedicated to St Lawrence and Our Lady, and formed from a trio of cottages on the

29 *Ibid.*, pp. 440–1.

30 See for a listing, F. Danner (ed.), *Catalogus totius Sacri, Candudi, Canonici ac Exempti Ordinis Praemonstratensis ineunte anno 1894* (Innsbruck, 1894), pp. 102–4. For the Tongerlo missions at the same date, see the same work at pp. 55–6. A historical perspective on the houses, including those (the overwhelming majority) no longer existing, is offered in Norbert Backmund, *Monasticon Praemonstratense* (Straubing: Attenkofersche Buchdruckerei, 1949–56, 3 vols., revised edition Berlin and New York: Walter de Gruyter, 1983).

31 This should probably be ascribed to administrative rationalization. Both Ullathorne and Ilsley were efficient administrators: see Mary McInally, *Edward Ilsley, Bishop of Birmingham 1888–1911, Archbishop of Birmingham 1911–1921* (London: Burns Oates, 2002), p. 77 (Ullathorne) and p. 400 (Ilsley as 'consolidating' and 'courageously readjusting' the work of Ullathorne and others).

32 *Rapport sur nos maisons d'Angleterre, 1895*. Frigolet Archives, Cartons Storrington, E29, p. 22. This did not mean there was no need for alms: The January 1892 issue of the Frigolet journal included an appeal which used the rather strong term 'indigence': 'La Mission de Bedworth (Angleterre)', *Cour d'honneur de Marie. Annales Norbertines*, 29/337, pp. 91–2.

Leicester Road.³³ Served at first from Nuneaton, by secular clerics or Friars Minor, Ilsley invited the Storrington canons, or more specifically, François Laborde of Weston, to take their place, not as visiting clergy but as resident pastors on site.

Over the next twenty-three years, Laborde proved an indefatigable and effective worker. As the historian of Catholic Bedworth remarks, 'this little French priest led a simple, mortified, self-sacrificing life, only getting for himself the bare essentials in food and clothing. It was by work and prayer he obtained the money to build the glorious work he accomplished.'³⁴ (Careful account books of the 'money', in both French and English, are retained in the Muston Archives.) Making Bedworth his centre—it was a town, rather than village or hamlet, hence the transfer of the mission house from Weston in 1892, Laborde both expanded the church he inherited and built from nothing a presbytery, school, and what would later be called 'social housing'.

He also started a custom, later continued at Storrington (and, subsequently, Muston), of annual novenas to what seems at first sight a rather unlikely trio of saints: Norbert (novena from 6–14 June), Francis Xavier (novena from 4–12 March), and Peter of Alcantara (novena from 11 to 19 October), though all of them could perhaps be classified as itinerant preachers, as well as workers of miracles. This, evidently, was the high point of the petitionary 'prayer' noted by Arthur Wall in *Some Bedworth Catholic History*. A triptych based on this threesome, painted for Storrington's Golden Jubilee and the consecration of its church in 1959 by the Chichester artist David O'Connell (1898–1976), is now at St Mary's Priory, Muston.³⁵ The novena continues to the present day (2023).

33 Arthur G. Wall, *Some Bedworth Catholic History* (Birmingham: The Shakespeare Press, nd), pp. 7–9. Muston Archives.

34 *Ibid.*, p. 16.

35 Though the iconography for this side-altar panel painting was provided with an elaborate explanation of its own for which the central theme was given as 'conflict against evil, led by three Saints but dominated by the elevated Host' (the Shrine of Our Lady of England, Storrington, *The St Norbert Triptych*, Muston Archives), the vicar-general of Southwark wrote on 3 December 1959 to the canons protesting in the name of Bishop Cyril Cowderoy, both as to the design ('his Lordship did not like the painting, as it appeared in the photograph'), and to its installation without his consent ('the Bishop was surprised, and, indeed, displeased to find that the Triptych was already in position when he made his Visitation on 27th October'), Letter of [Revd.} J. A. Callahan to C. H. Mathee, CRP (Hubert Mathee was the last Tongerlo canon to be prior of Storrington before the independence of the canonry from the Belgian abbey was conceded in 1962). His response was evidently satisfactory since Cowderoy wrote personally to Prior Mathee on Christmas Eve, 1959, denying that he had serious aesthetic (or theological) objections to the work and adding, 'It will be in order to have it', Letter of 24 December 1959 from Bishop Cyril Cowderoy to

In 1912 Laborde went as prior to Storrington, and as an obituary published on his death in 1930 commented: 'The extensive plans he had in mind for Weston never matured. His attention had soon to be diverted, in the main, to Bedworth, and the Weston scheme was eventually transferred to Storrington where, in his hands, it not only took shape, but at the time of his death was well on the way to a noble completion.'[36] The attempt to do so was expensive. In 1904/5 the canons were seeking to secure a nominal retraction of any claim to diocesan ownership of 'Arden Lodge'—a house, with adjacent field, built by a convert clergyman and earlier acquired by the Administrator of Frigolet, Denis Bonnefoy (administrator 1893–9 before a very brief abbacy of a few months prior to his death). This anxiety about title deeds did not portend a renewed commitment to Weston, for the aim was simply to render the property saleable, deemed necessary to prevent the collapse of Storrington once the French State, under the anti-clerical warlord (and former seminarian) Emile Combes (1835–1921), had seized Frigolet's capital assets. In any case, by the opening years of the twentieth century Weston Hall had passed into Protestant hands. The de Barys' successors, it was thought, would leap at the chance to extend their holdings. But in the end Arden Lodge was purchased by a devout family immensely supportive of the parish, a preferable solution.[37] Archbishop Ilsley's lawyers were warned that, in the nature of things, repaying the diocese could not be a priority.[38] Finance at the Frigolet Storrington was always of the hand-to-mouth variety.

From 1892 to 1927 Weston-in-Arden was served from Bedworth. In the middle of that period—in 1912, to be precise—a change-over from the Premonstratensians to the diocesan clergy dispelled another Frigolet dream.[39] When in 1923 the Bedworth church was finally consecrated, the only Norbertine present was Philip Beasley-Suffolk (1879–1940), son of one of the original four Recusant families, the Beasleys of Griff.[40] He would in time be the last canon of the Frigolet succession at Storrington itself. An alert observer, Xavier de Fourvière Rieux, had opined that Weston-in-Arden, or the adjacent Bedworth, owing to their central position in England, would actually have offered a better basis for future Premonstratensian life and expansion than Storrington, in sleepy West Sussex, ever could.[41] But it was not to be.

the Prior of Storrington. Both letters are in the Muston Archives.

36 B. Hickson, *Obituary Notice of Francis Laborde*. Muston Archives.
37 *Our Lady of the Sacred Heart, Weston-in-Arden*, pp. 26, 34–6.
38 *Anonymous Notes*. Muston Archives.
39 Wall, *Some Bedworth Catholic History*, p. 16.
40 *Ibid.*, p. 19.
41 Thus ran the recommendation in the official report commissioned by the

From the Midlands, my overview proceeds now to the Northern counties—from Warwickshire to Westmorland, in fact. Ambleside, at the northern tip of Windermere, might be thought an inspired choice, at any rate for lovers of the English Lakes, and devotees of the Romantic Movement, when a Premonstratensian foundation emerged there, by an unusual method, in 1890.[42] The proximity of the site of the former Norbertine monastery at Shap (by Haweswater in the Central Lakes) naturally suggested for this further Frigolet venture the name of 'Shap Cell'.

There was a pre-history to the canons' presence, albeit of a patchy kind. The anonymous author of a 'Historical Sketch of the Catholic Church at Ambleside' found reason to believe that Benedictine monks in the Cumbrian missions occasionally celebrated Mass in local hotels. That may be no more than surmise, based on the exponential growth of tourism in the Lake District from the 1860s onwards combined with local knowledge of the proximity of the Benedictine parishes along the Cumberland coast. According to Eleanor Davidson, in her short history of a parish further down the Lake at Bowness, the only known resident Catholic family in Ambleside were the Bonneys who 'may certainly be considered the founder Catholic family in the district'.[43] Richard Bonney, a Lytham man, educated by the Jesuits at Stonyhurst College, had come to Ambleside at some date prior to 1834 and married a Prot-estant girl from nearby Sawrey. In 1879 a secular canon of the Hexham diocese, Luke Curry (1816–90) of Dodding Green, Skelmergh, the oldest Catholic mission in Westmorland (in use as a centre of operation by the Northern District's Vicars Apostolic since the late seventeenth century), began a practice of coming over to Ambleside by horse and trap. At least in the summer months, he rented a room for the purpose of a Mass-house in 'Skelton's print shop in Church Street'.[44] But with growing competition for commercial space, the price for this shop-oratory ('St

Administrator of Frigolet, Denis Bonnefoy, as cited by Ardura, *L'Abbaye Saint-Michel de Frigolet*, p. 77, on the basis of the original manuscript in the Frigolet Archives, Cartons 'Storrington', E29.

42 The hard-headed author of the *Rapport sur nos maisons d'Angleterre, 1895*. Frigolet Archives, Cartons Storrington, E29, p. 47 was struck by the ambient beauty: 'Ambleside is an enchanted countryside, a smiling corner of Switzerland transported into England'.

43 Eleanor Davidson, 'The Story of the Parish [of St Herbert at Windermere]', p. 4. Typescript in Ambleside Catholic Parish archives. An expanded version of this TS was printed in 1983 as *Our Lady of Windermere and St Herbert. The Story of a Parish* and updated in 1999 under the same title.

44 'Historical Sketch of the Catholic Church at Ambleside', *The Parishioner* 14/9 (1934), pp. 21–3, and here at p. 21.

Joseph's Chapel') became exorbitant and he withdrew. Another attempt at gathering a Catholic congregation was made when Elizabeth Anne Aglionby (1815–78), convert member of an ancient Cumberland family, rented nearby Belmount Hall. Situated between Ambleside and Hawkshead, the property would later be owned by Beatrix Potter (1866–1943), the children's writer and illuminator. With gentry confidence, Aglionby threw open to the public, much to the landowner's chagrin, a private chapel served by her own chaplain. But soon her efforts were re-directed to helping found the Catholic parish in Coniston village where John Ruskin (1819–1900) aided her efforts by contributing the sanctuary window, albeit four years after her death.

In 1889 Joshua Bradley, a convert clergyman of means, made a new beginning of a less transient sort. Learning of the Mass-less condition of Catholics in Ambleside, he rented a house called Broadlands in 'The Borrans', where Ambleside touches Windermere at Waterhead. He also acquired at the Liverpool Exhibition (the 'International Exhibition of Navigation, Commerce and Industry' opened by Queen Victoria in Wavertree in 1886) a ready-for-use corrugated iron chapel which he erected in the grounds.

Then in 1890 a second clergyman succeeded Bradley—and not of any conventional kind. Dunstan Sellon (1855–1925[?][45]) had made his novitiate as a *Prémontré* of the Congregation of France in 1887, in the early days of Storrington. But there was no evidence he had ever completed philosophical or theological studies. In 1889, doubtless on account of his relatively advanced age (at any rate, as an Ordination candidate of the period) the bishop of Southwark had, it seems, agreed to ordain him on condition that he 'remained *in claustro* to study and that he was not employed for any external ministry such as preaching or hearing confessions'.[46] Eight months later he arrived in the Hexham diocese where he was at once given the mission of Ambleside. He soon embarked on an ambitious scheme: the building of what the 'Historical Sketch' describes as a 'preparatory [Norbertine] house of studies' on the corner

45 He is presumed to have left the Norbertine Order on the closure of his foundation, thus Ardura, *L'Abbaye Saint-Michel de Frigolet*, p. 70. No death date is recorded in the Frigolet necrology. If he is to be identified with Marmaduke St Juste Sellon, who appears as a priest in the Westminster diocese (see below, footnote 256) from 1903 until 1925, he may perhaps be supposed to have died in that year.

46 *Rapport sur nos maisons d'Angleterre, 1895*, p. 41. Frigolet Archives, Cartons Storrington, E29. He was ordained a Catholic priest on 21 September 1889: information received through the kindness of the Revd John Butters, formerly of Ushaw College, who visited Bishop's House in Newcastle to investigate historic copies of the *Northern Catholic Calendar* on my behalf. At the time of writing, the diocesan archives are closed, awaiting rehousing.

of two roads, Lake Road and Wansfell Road, in the Lakeland town. It should be explained that Lake Road is the principal thoroughfare of Ambleside, joining the town with the edge of Windermere. Wansfell Road, which meets it at a right angle, is where the replacement for the iron chapel—*Mater Amabilis* church, dating from 1933—stands today. In the same 'sketch', a retrospect from the 1930s, *The Parishioner* reported that stones from Shap Abbey were apparently used in the substantial construction.[47] 'Shap Cell' was certainly built of Lakeland stone of some provenance, as the present author noted during an exploratory visit on 18 April 2023. But then so are most larger houses of a certain age in Ambleside.

In July 1892 the bishop of Hexham and Newcastle—Thomas William Wilkinson (1825–1909), the fifth bishop—was invited to bless the foundation stone, and to confirm both children and recent converts.[48] The stone he laid is still visible, bearing the Premonstratensian motto *Ad omne opus bonum paratum* ('ready for every good work'). He was evidently ready, at first, to take at face value Dunstan Sellon's prediction of a solid future for the sons of St Norbert in the Lakes. Described as a 'north-country Tory ... disinclined to radical change', Wilkinson doubtless sympathized politically, as well as ecclesiastically, with the plight of Religious attached—however loosely—to French monasteries at the mercy of an anti-clerical Republican regime.[49] But the bishop was soon disabused, chiefly owing to the educational limitations of the school where Sellon was sole master. When, in the course of his survey of the English and Scottish missions of Frigolet, Xavier de Fourvière Rieux visited Bishop Wilkinson at St Cuthbert's College, Ushaw, he found the bishop convinced that Sellon was 'incapable of directing an institution of secondary education', a judgment based on empirical evidence: he had 'not formed a single good student'.[50]

---

47 Muston Archives. In 1933 at least one stone from Shap was incorporated into the new church: or so reported *The Universe* for 8 September of that year. Cutting preserved in Ambleside Catholic Parish Archive. I am indebted to the Revd Bernard Partington, then parish priest, for access to these papers during my visit of 18 April 2023.

48 'Chronique', *Cour d'honneur de Marie. Annales Norbertines* 29/342 (1892), p. 144; 29/346 (1892), pp, 239–40.

49 Leo Gooch, 'Henry O'Callaghan: Manning's Reluctant Episcopal Protégé', in Sheridan Gilley (ed.), *Victorian Churches and Churchmen. Essays Presented to Vincent Alan McClelland* (Woodbridge: Boydell Press, 2005), pp. 58–74, and here at p. 73. (O'Callaghan was Wilkinson's predecessor; he lasted in the see of Hexham for only a year, most of which he spent *in absentia*, before retiring to Rome and Florence.)

50 *Rapport sur nos maisons d'Angleterre, 1895*, p. 60. Frigolet Archives, Cantons Storrington, E29.

On the basis of his correspondence in the Frigolet Archives, Sellon might give every appearance of being a radical individualist. Yet *The Universe and Catholic Times* recalled in retrospect how, on the occasion of the episcopal stone-laying, 'White Canons' had been seen to 'come from all over England to witness the pathetic opening of a little iron church on a tiny plot of land'.[51] It would be interesting to know whether canons from the Tongerlo foundations were sufficiently ecumenical to attend this Frigolet event. (The Order proper, and the Primitive Observance Congregation of France were not yet one body.) Alas, the guest list, if such were drawn up, does not survive.

That invaluable Muston source, *News Cuttings*, contains a notable advertisement placed in an unidentified broadsheet in 1893, the year following the stone-laying of what Sellon, who had already started to receive postulants, evidently considered the future priory. 'St Norbert's Home School, Shap Cell, Ambleside' invited applications from parents of 'boys too young and backward for the ordinary College course'.[52] The model, no doubt, was the 'juvénat' at Frigolet itself, where the school was intended not only for the sons of unusually devout parents but as a seed-ground for future vocations. The advertisement was successful, though in the event 'Shap Cell' would later become firstly the 'Wansfell Tower Hotel' and subsequently 'Wansfell Tower Court', a set of seven self-contained apartments. A severe judge, Xavier de Fourvière Rieux, unsympathetic to Dunstan Sellon's initiatives and determined, if at all possible, to nip them in the bud, had to confess that, confronted with the boys, he was 'edified by their good behaviour in the house and in church. Dressed in white, as our *maîtrisiens* at Frigolet used to be, they acquitted themselves with zeal and piety in their little functions as cantors, ceremonialists, and servers at Mass'.[53] But this moment of weakness soon passed.

Not that Sellon's work was restricted to the educational scheme for which a special blessing from Pope Leo XIII was obtained on 12 March 1893. Sellon 'went far afield in his spiritual ministrations', saying Mass at Keswick for some hundred Catholics and at Thirlspot on Thirlmere for approximately two hundred Catholic navvies employed in converting that lake to its present use, courtesy of the Manchester Water Works.[54]

51 *The Universe and Catholic Times*, for 17 September 1892. Cutting preserved in Ambleside Catholic Parish Archive.

52 *News Cuttings*, p. 51. Muston Archives.

53 *Rapport sur nos maisons d'Angleterre, 1895*, p. 48. Frigolet Archives, Cartons Storrington, E28.

54 'Historical Sketch of the Catholic Church at Ambleside', p. 22. The controverted transformation of Thirlmere is described in Ian Francis, Stuart Holmes and Bruce Yardley, *The Lake District. Landscape and Geology* ((Crowwood Presss, Ramsbury,

These, of course, were just the kind of people the owner of Belmount Hall feared Miss Aglionby would introduce into his drawing-room. The ethnicity of the navvies was pertinent. Beatrix Potter had her anxieties on that score. 'There is not much unemployment about here [Ambleside], but things are very bad at Barrow; and there are Irish there which is a certain amount [of] risk according to the police.'[55]

It was unfortunate for Sellon that the 1893 crisis at Frigolet which rendered untenable the position of Paulin Boniface deprived him of an abbot who — to say the least — valued initiative and replaced him with an 'Administrator' keen to re-introduce seemly order into (what he considered) the state of semi-anarchy he had inherited. In June of that year, Sellon wrote to Bonnefoy to give an account of his ways. With a tacit admission that his creation of not just a school but a house of postulants stood on slightly shaky ground, he explained to Bonnefoy that 'Father Paulinus had permitted me to begin a little novitiate to prepare some children for the Order'. He expressed the hope, perhaps not entirely honestly, to see the Administrator someday soon at Ambleside. But as so often in mission correspondence the principal request was financial. Though the Duke of Norfolk and an 'amiable benefactress' had helped, new needs were pressing.[56] And indeed the 'Historical Sketch' reports that an urgent appeal for funds was shortly to be published in *The Lamp*, for the iron chapel was deemed to be unsafe in winter.[57] For the moment, some money at least was forthcoming,[58] but the future Abbot Bonnefoy was increasingly concerned about his remotely situated subject. In a letter of 24 July 1894 he expressed alarm at a newspaper article published over the Premonstratensian post-nominal letters 'CRP', predecessor to the later twentieth-century 'O.Praem.' It was written by a former Passionist to whom, seemingly, Setton had given the Norbertine habit.[59] Mounting anxieties about Ambleside were never allayed, and

Marlborough, 2022), 136–7.

55 Letter of 4 March 1921 from Beatrix Potter (Mrs Heelis) to her publisher Fruing and Warne, cited in Donald M. MacRaild, *Culture, Conflict and Migration. The Irish in Victorian Cumbria* (Liverpool: Liverpool University Press, 1998), p. 209.

56 Letter of 20 June 1893 from Dunstan Sellon, O.Praem., to Denis Bonnefoy, O.Praem. Frigolet Archives, Cartons Storrington, E29.

57 More especially, the issue of 20 October 1894, *The Lamp* was a magazine founded by William Lockhart, IC (1820–92), rector of the Fathers of Charity at St Etheldreda's, Ely Place — a Tractarian convert, cousin to Walter Scott's son-in-law and biographer.

58 Letter of 15 August 1893 from Dunstan Sellon, O.Praem., to Denis Bonnefoy, O.Praem. Frigolet Archives, Cartons Storrington, E29.

59 Letter of 24 July 1894 from Denis Bonnefoy, O.Praem., to Dunstan Sellon, O.Praem. Frigolet Archives, Cartons Storrington, E29.

within eighteen months Bonnefoy had cut the Gordian knot by formally suppressing the Westmorland house. In his chastened response, Sellon claimed he had in any case 'long cherished the desire to have a dispensation in order to be united with the Premonstratensians [i. e. the historic Order] at Tongerlo or otherwise be under the obedience of the abbot-general at Strahov [this at a time before abbots-general, only recently re-invented, lived at Rome]'.[60] But relations soon deteriorated after François Laborde — acting, evidently, as Bonnefoy's intermediary — wrote from Bedworth to insist that the Shap Cell school be closed forthwith and the parents notified to take their children away. Bonnefoy had spoken critically of Sellon's 'egoism' but. in the light of this *ukaz* from Bedworth, the word, which may have hit its mark, elicited a sardonic riposte. There was surely no need to come so far north in order to observe that particular character-trait: it would suffice to end the journey from Frigolet half-way — with the obvious implication that the Forest of Arden sheltered a local superior richly endowed with the quality in question.[61]

Sellon's hope now turned on entering the novitiate of the Canons Regular of the Lateran,[62] which may have recommended itself as a solution not just to his own vocational problem but as a possible way to salvage his school. Under English law there was a possibility the school might be deemed his personal property. Certainly he did not give up without a struggle. Though the 'Historical Sketch' computed his date of final departure as 1900, Eileen Stanning, in *A Short History of Mater Amabilis, Ambleside*, is closer to the mark when she gives the last year of his residence as 1898.[63] That year the *Northern Catholic Calendar* recorded his replacement by two Canons Regular of the Lateran, whose mission was, however, even more short-lived than his own. In 1899 the church of Mater Amabilis, Ambleside, is described laconically as 'served from Windermere'.[64] *The Catholic Directory, Ecclesiastical*

60 Letter of 2 December 1895 from Dunstan Sellon, O.Praem., to Denis Bonnefoy, O. Pream. Frigolet Archives, Cartons Storrington, E29.

61 Letter of 10 December 1895 from Dunstan Sellon, O.Praem., to Denis Bonnefoy, O.Praem. Frigolet Archives, Cartons Storrington, E29.

62 Letter of 16 March 1896 from Dunstan Sellon, O.Praem., to Denis Bonnefoy, O.Praem. Frigolet Archives, Cartons Storrington, E29.

63 Eileen Stanning, *A Short History of Mater Amabilis*, Ambleside, undated but after 1996. The photocopy in the Ambleside Catholic parish archive is unfortunately incomplete. The last issue of the *Catholic Directory* for Great Britain that finds Sellon at Ambleside dates from the previous year: *The Catholic Directory, Ecclesiastical Register and Almanac for the Year of Our Lord 1897* (London: Burns, Oates, & Co., 1897), p. 165.

64 Information received from the former editor of that journal of record, the Revd John Butters.

Register and Almanac finds Sellon himself attached in those years to the Cornish house of the Canons Regular of the Lateran in Bodmin—thus explaining, by association, the brief sojourn of members of that body in the Lakes.[65] The arrival of the Canons of the Lateran proved not to be the prelude of a new dispensation. Rather was it a postlude to Frigolet's short-lived 'Shap Cell'.

65 I am inclined to identify Dunstan Sellon with the 'Marmaduke St. Juste Sellon' who in later issues of the *Catholic Directory* (1903–25) appears at different venues in the Westminster archdiocese. There is a distinctly 'Firbankian' note in this name (after Ronald Firbank, 1886–1926), not to say, indeed, a possible echo of Frederick Rolfe, Baron Corvo (1860–1913), a nearer contemporary.

～ 8 ～

North of the Border:
Whithorn and Beyond

U NDER THE IRREPRESSIBLE ABBOT BONIFACE Frigolet canons also
looked north of the Anglo-Scottish Border. Perhaps they were
conscious of the historic resonances of the 'Auld Alliance', reaching back as it did to the thirteenth century, and specifically to the treaty
signed by John Balliol and Philip IV in 1295, renewed by all French kings
(except Louis XI) until sunk by the Scottish Reformation in 1560.[1] In 1889
a Marquess of Bute who was himself an avowed Scottish Nationalist
proposed to fund a return to Scotland of an Order whose mother house
had been unmistakably French (the arms of the Order feature the fleur-
de-lys of the Kings of France). More specifically, he planned for them
to return to Whithorn, the historic site that, between the thirteenth and
sixteenth centuries, had been, for the mediaeval Scots among them, their
pride and boast. Close by the legendary Cave of Ninian, a Norbertine
priory had furnished the cathedral chapter of the pre-Reformation see of
Galloway in the high Middle Ages.[2] In 1886/7 the Crichton-Stuart family
had paid for the architectural historian William Galloway (1830–97) to
carry out a major archaeological excavation and, to whatever degree
proved possible, a restoration of 'Whithorn Priory'.[3] Now the plan was

1 Norman Macdougall, *An Antidote to the English: The Auld Alliance, 1295–1560*
(East Linton: Tuckwell Press, 2001).
2 For the little that is known about the historical Ninian, see John T. Koch (ed.),
'Ninian, St.', in *Celtic Culture. A Historical Encyclopedia* (Santa Barbara, CA: ABC-
Clio, 2006), vol. IV, p. 1358. In 1177 Bishop Christian of Galloway had introduced
a colony of White Canons from the abbey of Soulseat near Stranraer: for the mediaeval Scottish Premonstratensians see Ian B. Cowan and David E. Easson, *Medieval
Religious Houses: Scotland, with an Appendix on the Houses in the Isle of Man* (London
and New York: Longmans, 1976, 2nd edition), pp. 100–4.
3 Anna Ritchie, 'From Colonsay to Whithorn: the work of a 19th century antiquary, William Galloway', *Proceedings of the Society of Antiquaries of Scotland* 142
(2013), pp. 435–356.

for any revived buildings to be suitably inhabited by—what else?—Premonstratensians. And the Frigolet diaspora was available.

The Frigolet canons were provisionally to be housed in a presbytery, re-named by them 'St Norbert's Priory', with responsibility for the parish of the Sacred Heart, Wigtown, the county town of the homonymous Scottish shire, bordered as the latter is by the Irish Sea and the Solway Firth to the west and south, with Ayrshire to the north and the Stewartry of Kirkcudbright to the east. The Wigtown church had been opened a decade previously, in 1869, and was served by the clergy of the 'Western District' (under the governance of a Vicar Apostolic) until in 1878 the mediaeval diocese of Galloway was re-created, along with other Pre-Reformation Scottish circumscriptions, by Pope Leo XIII.

But the real target for the canons was Whithorn itself. In 1880 *The Catholic Directory for the Clergy and Laity of Scotland* had complained that, at the historic site of St Ninian's *Candida Casa*, 'Mass is said in a rented hall, which for wretchedness and want of comfort has few equals in Scotland', noting that 'as far as local resources are concerned, nothing can be done towards providing suitable accommodation'.[4] In 1882, the editor of the *Directory* was able to report that '[t]his state of things, doubly disgraceful in the city and see of St Ninian, has been put an end to by the influence and liberality of the Marquis of Bute'.[5] Three acres of land had been secured in an area of the town once owned by the Pre-Reformation bishops. 'On a future day, it is hoped, a sanctuary may here be raised not unworthy of the ancient Cathedral whose ruins are near. But for the present the wants of the Whithorn Catholics have been abundantly met by the erection of an elegant and commodious iron Chapel built in the most substantial and solid style of which such a structure is capable'.[6] This construction, a preliminary to glories to come, was dedicated to a trio of saints: Ninian, Martin, and John.[7]

Notice of the Frigolet foundation at Wigtown/Whithorn first appears in *The Catholic Directory for the Clergy and Laity of Scotland, 1890* where

4 *The Catholic Directory for the Clergy and Laity of Scotland, 1880* (Edinburgh: Chisholm, 1880), p. 117.

5 *The Catholic Directory for the Clergy and Laity of Scotland, 1882* (Edinburgh: Chisholm, 1882), p. 200.

6 *Ibid.*

7 'Trio of saints': the Galwegian see of St Ninian, the 'apostle of the Southern Picts', had been dedicated to St Martin of Tours. The name of St John the Evangelist was added to honour the first bishop of Galloway in the restored hierarchy, this being John McLachlan's *onomasticon*. The chapel did eventually have a successor of sorts: the church of SS Martin and Ninian built in George Street to a design by H. S. Goodhart-Rendel (1887–1959) at the end of the 1950s (and subsequently rather ruthlessly reordered).

the canons are in charge both in the parish church (Wigtown) and at the chapel-of-ease (Whithorn), while, so the information provided runs, forays were made on an occasional basis to the fishing village of Portwilliam, outlet to the sea for local farm produce—or more specifically to Elrig, a nearby clachan or hamlet best known in a subsequent century as the birthplace of the author and naturalist Gavin Maxwell (1914–69).[8] By 1892 the canons were also acting as chaplains to an agricultural training school for orphans, erected on a farm at Criagiach in the moorland district of Kirkcowan—once again, through the generosity of Lord Bute.[9] Perhaps non-coincidentally, Kirkcowan lay across the mediaeval pilgrim route to Whithorn Priory.

Though episcopal support was a necessary condition, the crucial figure in the arrival of Frigolet canons in North Britain was indeed Bute himself: John Patrick Crichton Stuart, the third Marquess (1847–1900), noted antiquarian and Catholic convert.[10] As his most recent biographer explains, 'Bute had spent a few happy days at the end of 1888 "digging" for ancient ecclesiastical remains at Whithorn, and he had organized, although not attended, a celebration of the saint's life in that area. Now in 1889 he funded the setting up of a new foundation.'[11] His preference was to cloak with discretion his personal involvement, and to work, at least initially, through the bishop. That would mean the first bishop of Galloway in the restored hierarchy, John McLachlan (1826–93), who was now to be presented as an enthusiast for the Premonstratensian project. The *Catholic Times* reported on 30 August that year, 'The Right Rev. Dr. McLachlan, the present Bishop of Galloway, had long cherished the desire to make a link between the present and the past of his diocese, by inviting the monks [sic] of Prémontré to return to the diocese in which their predecessors once so successfully laboured'.[12]

But a copied letter in the Muston Archives makes it plain that the initial proposal was in reality Bute's own and was actually made not to canons of Frigolet at all, but to the canons of Tongerlo already present in

8 *The Catholic Directory for the Clergy and Laity of Scotland, 1890* (Edinburgh: Aberdeen University Press, 1890), pp. 134–5.

9 *The Catholic Directory for the Clergy and Laity of Scotland, 1892* (Aberdeen: A. King & Co., 1892), p. 163.

10 Rosemary Hannah, *The Grand Designer: Third Marquess of Bute* (Edinburgh: Birlinn, 2012). The third Marquess of Bute was also the eighth Earl of Dumfries, with large landholdings in south-west Scotland as well as in South Wales and elsewhere.

11 Hannah, *The Grand Designer*, p. 270. The Bute Archive at Mount Stuart includes letters in 1885 from Herbert Maxwell and R. W. Cochran Patrick reporting on the progress of excavations at the site (BU/21/214), and from William Galloway on the same topic in 1890 (BU/21/274, BU/21/275).

12 *Catholic Times*, 30 August 1889, in Hannah, *The Grand Designer*, pp. 270–1.

the East of England (see Chapter 3 above). The letter in question is dated well before the aristocratic archaeologist's exploits in 1888. Early in 1883, the 'episcopus Candidae Casae', as McLachlan described himself, wrote from the pro-cathedral in Dumfries to Prior Geudens at Crowle about a plan that was hatching. It was, he insisted, a scheme to be 'discussed' rather than, once communicated, to be 'regarded as settled'. 'His Lordship', he wrote, with reference to Bute, 'has had some idea of building a Cathedral at Whithorn for the present diocese and Bishop of Galloway and it has been suggested that perhaps a body of Premonstratensians might be got to serve it'.[13] Certainly, the bishop explained, absent some such unusual, if historically appropriate, innovation, there would be in south-west Scotland no secular clerics available to sing cathedral offices. But the prior must be warned that canons regular, if they came, would have no rights vis-à-vis any eventual secular chapter of canons, nor would they have a role in regard to the election of the bishop or any claim to proprietorship of the cathedral. Moreover, they could expect no financial subsidy from the diocese, while the few local Catholics (estimated at twenty families), all being 'labourers', could hardly do much to support them. Nor could they hope to raise monies from the surrounding missions all of which were strapped for cash. Any funds they might acquire from the people they served would have to be found in the immediate vicinity for which they would be directly responsible. 'The Religious would have to take the spiritual charge of the Catholics in Whithorn and in the surrounding country within a line to be drawn about half way between Whithorn and Wigtown.' The offer was hardly enticing and it is unsurprising that no positive reply was received.

But the Marquess was not so easily thwarted, and the coincidence of the expulsions from Frigolet some five years later—together, no doubt, with the still fresh memory of those 'happy days' on the dig in 1888—played into his hands. In February 1889 Louis de Gonzague Daras wrote to Bute from Weston-in-Arden. Abbot Boniface had asked him to respond to the Marquess' generous offer to re-found Whithorn priory. He lets fall that Bute had already contributed financially to both Storrington and Weston.[14] The letter would have impressed Bute with its author's antiquarian learning. Daras had visited Premonstratensian sites in Scotland during his six year sojourn in England and inspected pertinent charter material in libraries both in Britain and on the Conti-

13 Letter of 15 January 1883 from Bishop John (McLachlan) to Prior Geudens. Muston Archives.

14 Letter of 21 September 1889 from Louis Gonzague Daras, O.Praem., to Lord Bute. Bute Archives, BU/21/261. I am grateful to Lynsey Nairn, the Archivist of Mount Stuart, for her assistance before and during my enjoyable visit on 18 July 2023.

nent. Letters of April and May 1889 continued in the same erudite vein which must have pleased their scholarly recipient. Daras signalled his interest in the archeological work in progress at Whithorn and shared his knowledge of the ground-plans of English Premonstratensian abbeys.

On 3 July 1889 he was able to inform Bute that Bishop McLachlan had given the canons their mandate for the missions of both Wigtown and Whithorn. 'Here you have, my Lord, a charming occasion to rebuild the entire cathedral of Whithorn, but one mustn't speak of this to Mr [William] Galloway [Bute's overseer of the excavations at Whithorn], the good man would lose his head in his transports of joy'.[15] In the same month Daras undertook to interpret the episcopal mind on the Premonstratensian future. McLachlan 'desires that in the course of two years a monastery be constructed at Whithorn, to form novices and prepare missionaries'.[16] On 1 August Bute noted in his diary laconically but with satisfaction, 'Premonstratensians arrived at Wigtown'.[17]

On 6 August 1890 Daras wrote his first letter from 'St Norbert's Priory', in the Wigtownshire capital. 'I have disembarked with fifty cases of books and effects.' He was determined, so he told his patron, to create in Galloway an 'exact and perfect' example of the life of his Order. His human resources were, however, rather few: two priests, a deacon, and a postulant (a former teacher in a Jesuit college in the United States). Their first public appearance had taken the form of the celebration of Terce, Mass and Sext in the parish church. 'You would have been amazed, my Lord, to see the entire people follow unhesitatingly all the evolution and the movements of our liturgy. They rose, bowed, turned towards the altar, absolutely like a great monastic community and the general impression was striking (*prestigieuse*)'' Next Sunday, he explained, he would be initiating a similar 'installation' at Whithorn, and the following Sunday at Portwilliam 'though there is no church'.[18]

Not that the canons were necessarily well-equipped with liturgical paraphernalia for solemn worship. Later that month he requested from Bute a monstrance and pyx in which to hold the Sacrament, since placing the Host at the bottom of a chalice was scarcely seemly. These objects arrived in good time, by way of an Edinburgh jeweller, which suggests that they were not exactly commonplace examples of their kind.[19] In

15 Letter of 3 July 1889 from Louis de Gonzague Daras, O.Praem., to Lord Bute. Bute Archives, BU/21/261.

16 Letter of 23 July 1889 from Louis de Gonzague Daras, O.Praem., to Lord Bute. Bute Archives, BU/21/261.

17 Personal diary of John Patrick Crichton-Stuart. Bute Archives, BU/43/4.

18 Letter of 6 August 1889 from Louis de Gonzague Daras, O.Praem., to Lord Bute. Bute Archives, BU/21/272.

19 Letter of 1 September 1889 from Louis de Gonzague Daras, O.Praem., to Lord

early September he thanked Bute for the gift of bi-lingual books that would help the laity follow the Divine Office at both Wigtown and Whithorn. It would take, he wrote, an Order of canons regular like the Premonstratensians to 'make the faithful people acquire a taste for psalmody'.[20] In November he had to write again to thank him for the rest of the volumes of what he called the *Horae Breviarii Romani Latino-English*: presumably this was Bute's own translation.[21] Bute was always pleasantly surprised to hear when groups of Catholic laity, otherwise more accustomed to devotional manuals, were making use of it.

But the summer had not passed before Daras was giving thought to how to involve, in the outreach of the new foundation, Catholics from further afield. It was his intention, he told Bute, to ask the Holy See to erect an Archconfraternity of St Ninian with a plenary indulgence available for pilgrims on certain feast days. After all, there had been a time when 'the kings of Scotland and the people of Carlisle came thronging to Whithorn'.[22] The pilgrimages arranged by the Frigolet canons at Whithorn would be the one enduring feature of their efforts. Meanwhile others were starting to take notice. *The Catholic Directory for the Clergy and Laity of Scotland, 1890* reported that 'through the generosity of the Marquess of Bute the Premonstratensian Canons Regular have returned to Scotland after an absence of more than three hundred years, and into that part of the country where they flourished most before the Reformation'.[23] The editor of the *Directory* noted that Prior Daras (his Religious name quasi-Anglicized to 'Lewis Gonzaga'), had 'settled here', the canons having had 'confided to them the charge of the mission of Wigtown and the stations served from it'.[24] Some sounding of fanfares accompanied the event. On 11 September Daras wrote to Bute thanking him for the way that, on the feast of St Ninian, he had placed at the service of the Norbertines a choir from the Ayrshire town of Cumnock, which lay close by his second Scottish seat, Dumfries House.[25] Bute

Bute. Bute Archives, BU/21/261.

20 Letter of 5 September 1889 from Louis de Gonzague Daras, O.Praem., to Lord Bute. Bute Archives, BU/21/261.

21 Letter of 9 November 1889 from Louis de Gonzague Daras, O.Praem., to Lord Bute. Bute Archives, BU/21/261. In other words: *The Roman Breviary, reformed by order of the holy oecumenical Council of Trent, together with the offices since granted,* translated by John, marquess of Bute (Edinburgh: Blackwood, 1879), two volumes.

22 Letter of 29 August 1889 from Louis de Gonzague Daras, O.Praem., to Lord Bute. Bute Archives, BU/21/261.

23 *The Catholic Directory for the Clergy and Laity of Scotland, 1890*, p. 135.

24 *Ibid*.

25 Letter of 11 September 1889 from Louis de Gonzague Daras, O.Praem., to Lord Bute. Bute Archives, BU/21/261.

noted in his diary entry for 16 September, 'I heard afterwards that the festival of St Ninian at Whithorn for which the choir travelled through the night was brilliantly successful ... People of Whithorn seemingly much pleased by return of the Premonstratensian Order'.[26]

Daras was hoping to put his literary skills to the aid of the project. He shared with Bute his plan to write a popular, but researched, book on the saints of Scotland. It was a pity he did not have continuing access to the British Museum Library, 'the celebrated British Museum, the premier literary arsenal of the globe, which I had made my Paradise'. It 'still causes me bitter regret not to be able any longer to study there'.[27] But a month later he had discovered Glasgow's Mitchell Library and was equally enthused. 'What intellectual pleasure is procured by the sight of 150, 000 volumes classified in incomparable order and with a perfect catalogue'.[28] These claims to serious reading were not trumpery. Daras' correspondence with Bute shows how the Scottish peer used him to trace, through intermediaries, documents in French archives relevant to the story of the Catholic Church in Scotland while for his part Daras sought to bring to Bute's attention French-language works on art history and archaeology that might have escaped his notice. He exchanged notes about Scottish liturgical texts from the mediaeval period, the twelfth-century Norbertine author Adam of Dryburgh ('Adam the Scot'), and illuminated manuscripts. Daras was genuinely learned on Premonstratensian history, gathering materials over a lifetime for a *Bullarium Praemonstratense*, or as he explained to Bute, a 'chronological series of the pontifical acts in favour of our Order, from the twelfth to the nineteenth centuries'.[29]

Shortly after the move to Whithorn, an unfortunate scandal set back the foundation. Bute was seriously irritated to learn of a scene of a scene on the streets of Wigtown where three Premonstratensians, two postulants and a priest, had come publicly to blows. Prior Daras (though the title was contested by no less than his own abbot[30])

26 Personal diary of John Patrick Crichton-Stuart. Bute Archives, BU/43/4.

27 Letter of 13 November 1889 from Louis de Gonzague Daras, O.Praem., to Lord Bute. Bute Archives, BU/21/261.

28 Letter of 9 December 1889 from Louis de Gonzague Daras, O.Praem., to Lord Bute. Bute Archives, BU/21/261.

29 Letter postmarked 14 June 1890 from Louis de Gonzague Daras, O.Praem., to Lord Bute. Bute Archives, BU/21/272.

30 Letter of 21 March 1890 from Abbot Paulin Boniface to Louis de Gonzague Daras, O.Praem: 'You take the title "prior", but this must be properly understood: it is in the sense of superior but not of priory. Unless you have a house of your own, as at Farnborough and Storrington, your mission is only a mission. You are a superior of missionaries and not a prior in the strict sense of the word'. Frigolet

dismissed the postulants, and asked Abbot Boniface to send a suitable English-speaking replacement for the priest.[31] Bute warned Daras against the noxious effects of Scotch whiskey and expressed the wish that the offending priest—rather hopefully named for St Ninian and seemingly a Glaswegian with a chequered pre-Norbertine past—be forbidden from setting foot ever again on Scottish soil.[32] The *Catholic Directory* for 1890, in its catalogue of clergy, furnishes for the pugilistic canon the missing surname of 'Crawford'. With the publication of the 1891 successor volume he vanishes. Seemingly, the noble lord had got his way.[33] The Daras-Bute correspondence preserved at Mount Stuart confirms that this was so. In late October 1890 Daras was able to report to Bute that he had personally driven the priest to Girvan on his way to a period of therapeutic incarceration in the Trappist monastery of Mount Melleray (in Ireland's County Waterford).[34] Like many victims of alcoholism, Crawford had been adept at covering up his addiction, ostentatiously drinking only water at table and keeping in his cell, if not on his person, an impressive display of instruments of penance: hair-shirts, the discipline (a rope made of string studded with pieces of metal), and iron chains.[35] But the rat escaped the trap. At the end of the month Daras announced that Crawford had left Glasgow not for an Irish monastery but for the European Continent, a 'relief for Scotland'.[36] The episode seems to have demoralized Prior Daras, who in a plaintive self-accusatory letter, ascribed to his advanced age and the negative effect of his ecclesiastical trials his failures in governance of the priory.[37] Certainly the case did not impress his abbot. 'We have had only too many scandals for some time in England [*sic*]'.[38] A few weeks later, Paulin Boniface wrote to say there must be no more talk of novices

Archives, Cartons Storrington, E29.

31 Letters of 28 August and 4 September from Louis de Gonzague Daras, O.Praem., to Lord Bute. Bute Archives BU/21/272.

32 *Anonymous Notes*. Muston Archives.

33 *The Catholic Directory for the Clergy and Laity of Scotland, 1890*, p. 134; contrast: *The Catholic Directory for the Clergy and Laity of Scotland, 1891* (Aberdeen: A. King & Co.), pp. 165–74.

34 Letter of 21 October 1890 from Louis de Gonzague Daras, O.Praem., to Lord Bute. Bute Archives, BU/21/272.

35 *Ibid.*, and Letter of 23 October 1890 from Louis de Gonzague Daras, O.Praem., to Lord Bute. Bute Archives, BU/21/272.

36 Letter of 31 October 1890 from Louis de Gonzague Daras, O.Praem., to Lord Bute. Bute Archives, BU/21/272.

37 Letter of 23 August 1890 from Louis de Gonzague Daras, O.Praem., to Lord Bute. Bute Archives, BU/21/272.

38 Letter of 24 September 1890 from Abbot Paulin Boniface to Louis de Gonzague Daras, O.Praem. Frigolet Archives, Cartons Storrington, E29.

at Whithorn, 'neither English [sic] nor French'. The letter-writer had a respectably Ultramontane reason to hand. The only novitiate permitted by Rome was at Storrington, and 'we must all obey the Holy See despite the inconveniences that will result from our obedience', words which may attest some awareness that Scotland was not, after all, England.[39]

Clearly there was a need for prayer for the fledgling foundation, and not for current ills alone. It is not difficult to see how the coming of the canons fitted congruously into local hopes for a renaissance of the 'White House', home of the Apostle of the Southern Picts, and a revival of Catholic life in the surrounding countryside and towns. But Daras had set his sights higher still. The priory, as its official notepaper made clear, was now the home of 'St Ninian's Society for the Conversion of Scotland'. In March 1890 he reported that the primate of All Ireland had agreed to the formation in the diocese of Armagh of an 'union de prières pour l'Écosse'.[40] In April 1890, a flyer appeared for the Society, from which it transpired that the prayers in question were 'indulgenced' not only by the Irish primate (and the two Scottish archbishops, as well as the bishop of Galloway) but also by the pope. This 'Norbertine confraternity', as a testimonial from one of a number of 'priest-mission-aries' described it, was to publish a monthly review entitled, somewhat cryptically, *Scotland's Liberation*. Sending the first issue to Bute, Daras contended that Whithorn was a 'place of liberation' although in the current 'epoch of advanced civilization' the chains of idolatry from which the fourth-century bishop freed the pagan Southern Picts are replaced by those of the various Protestant denominations.[41] A list of 'Contributors and Fellow-Writers', along with appropriate topics for articles, was drawn up for this apostolic purpose.[42] A fine embossed image of 'St Ninian, Apostle and first Bishop of Galloway', was produced for

39 Letter of 20 November 1890 from Abbot Paulin Boniface to Louis de Gonzague Daras, O.Praem. Frigolet Archives, Cartons Storrington, E29.

40 Letter of 7 March 1890 from Louis de Gonzague Daras, O.Praem., to Lord Bute. Bute Archives, BU/21/272.

41 Copy of *Scotland's Liberation* dispatched by Daras to Lord Bute from the Franciscan friary in Glasgow. Bute Archives, BU/21/261.

42 Copy in Bute Archives, BU/21/272. An earlier suggestion for the title was 'Galloway Magazine' or (an even less inspired choice) 'Galloway Museum', an inappropriate transfer to English of the French term 'Muséon', meaning any place associated with sites of learning, Letter of 9 November 1889 from Louis de Gonzague Daras, O.Praem., to Lord Bute. Bute Archives, BU/21/261. The following year Daras proposed to change the title to 'The Messenger of Whithorn', since, after all, the publication's main aim was to 'make known news of the sanctuary to those who unite themselves to the Religious, praying continually for the Candida Casa', Letter of 13 October 1890 from Louis de Gonzague Daras, O.Praem., to Lord Bute. Bute Archives, BU/21/272. This was at any rate more realistic.

the pious contemplation of the Society's members, with, on its reverse side, prayers in his honour from the Proper of Saints of the Arbuthnott Missal, the only extant liturgical text of the mediaeval Scottish Use.[43]

In the course of 1890 'St Norbert's Priory' re-located to a property of Bute's, High Mains Farm, in Whithorn itself. On 15 July 1890 Daras had written to the landowner at Falkland Palace (another of his Scottish addresses), lamenting the present Wigtown siting of the priory. It was difficult to be the 'preachers of St Ninian' without having at Whithorn anywhere of their own to 'spend the night or deposit our things or our clothes'.[44] Bute's efficiency was evidently the equal of his generosity. Writing at the end of October 1890 Daras reported with satisfaction that, now ensconced on the sacred site, 'we begin tomorrow [1 November 1890] the Divine Office in choir for the Diocese and the Founders. May this *laus perennis* never be interrupted at Whithorn till the end of the ages'.[45] But doubtless the buildings were more akin in scale to the original Romano-British monastery than to its imposing high medieval Premonstratensian successor. 'The archeological remains from Whithorn suggest that the earliest buildings at the site included a modest rectangular cabin, painted white, ringed by wooden round houses ... The first monastery at Whithorn was small-scale and functional, more of a farmstead than a major ecclesiastical site.'[46] Yet (it could be countered) from acorns there do grow oaks.

Crichton-Stuart patronage, whether at Wigtown or at Whithorn, did not mean that the canons rested, financially, on their laurels. A 'Livre d'Or' for the 'monastery of Whithorn' preserved at Muston provides twelve printed lists of benefactors, encouraged to make a donation for 'notre nouvelle église': they ranged from Storrington parishioners to some of the great names of the English (or Welsh) Catholic families (Trafford, Clifford, Mostyn), from denizens of other Religious houses (including the Carthusians of Parkminster, also in exile) and a variety of English or Irish convents of nuns (Carmelites, Benedictines, Poor

43 Alexander Penrose Forbes (ed.), *Liber Ecclesiae beati Terrenani de Arbuthnott secundum usum Ecclesiae sancti Andreae in Scotia* (Burntisland: Pitsligo Press, 1864).

44 Letter of 15 July 1890 from Louis de Gonzague Daras, O.Praem., to Lord Bute. Bute Archives, BU/21/272.

45 Letter of 31 October 1890 from Louis de Gonzague Daras, O.Praem., to Lord Bute. Bute Archives, BU/21/272.

46 Janina Ramirez, *The Private Lives of Saints. Power, Passion and Politics in Anglo-Saxon England* (London: W. H. Allen, 2015), p. 81. There is justification for this author's including Ninian in a study of *English* history since in the 730s Whithorn became, with Hexham and Lindisfarne, a suffragan see of York: thus Frank M. Stenton, *Anglo-Saxon England* (Oxford: Oxford University Press, 1987, 3rd edition [= *Oxford History of England*, vol. II]), p. 109.

Clares, the Dominicanesses of Sienna Convent in Drogheda) or Sisters (including Mercy Convents, houses of the Congregation of the Holy Child Jesus, and the Institute of the Blessed Virgin Mary's establishment—the 'Bar Convent'—at York), as well as the abbots of Averbode and Leffe (Belgium), Jaszo, Siloë, and Schlägl (Austria-Hungary). Over time, the donors were increasingly French. They hailed especially from the Midi (Marseilles, Nimes, Aix) and the Basses-Alpes. The final list carries the names of twenty-two French benefactors, two from England, one from Ireland, and one from Wales. Judging by the balance-sheets provided, the gifts did not amount to the riches of Croesus (one anonymous donor described him- or, more likely, herself as 'A Poor Child'). But neither were they, in gross, insubstantial.[47]

By 1893, the priory had undergone a change of patronage, replacing 'Norbert' by 'Gilbert', a sign of a new regime, for Prior Daras had resigned and left Whithorn at Easter 1892 for Farnborough, dying there in early November of the same year.[48] The Gilbert in question was, surely, Gilbert of Neuffontaines (c. 1100–52), a former Crusader and later Premonstratensian abbot, rather than the better- known English saint, Gilbert of Sempringham (c. 1085–1189). The new dedication was presumably connected with a promised expansion heralded by *The Catholic Directory for the Clergy and Laity of Scotland, 1893*. There Scottish Catholics read that 'as the 'numbers of the community will be greatly increased in the early part of the year', priests would shortly become available to act as Retreat-masters, or to furnish help to the parochial clergy.[49] This was in addition to running an evidently already functioning 'Home School' where 'a few boys of delicate health receive instruction and special care under the immediate supervision of the Prior'.[50] But the expansion never occurred. Rather pathetically, the same announcement was made in 1894 and 1895, retaining the—by now anachronistic—phrase 'in the early part of the year'. The notice was suppressed for the 1896 edition of the *Directory*. By 1898 a secular priest was in charge again at Wigtown (the first time since 1889) and the Premonstratensians had disappeared entirely from the roll call of male Religious in the Galloway diocese. Bishop McLachlan had his doubts as early as 1890, considering Prior Daras, though a holy and humble man, to be lacking in the qualities needed for a new venture

47 *Livre d'Or, Monastery of Whithorn*. Muston Archives.

48 Letter of 13 November 1892 from Dean William Turner to Lord Bute. Bute Archives BU/21/306.

49 *The Catholic Directory for the Clergy and Laity of Scotland, 1893* (Aberdeen: A. King & Co., 1893), p. 174.

50 *Ibid.*, p. 173.

on the scale envisaged. He even wondered whether he might be on the verge of senility. At any rate, no other English-speaking canon had been available to take his place.[51] The considerable number of letters from Bishop McLachlan in the Frigolet Archives testify, however, to the care with which he had followed the venture at Whithorn.

In January 1896 the bishop of Galloway, now William Turner, the second bishop (1844–1914), wrote to Bute to say that the (Benedictine) abbot of Fort Augustus, Oswald Hunter-Blair (1853–1939), had suggested his community might take over the Whithorn priory. He was inclined to think that, with their substantial numbers, the Highland abbey should be allowed to try. Otherwise the property would revert to the possession of the Bute estate. 'I would much prefer them to another foreign experiment ... My experience with the people from Frigolet has made me rather diffident of success with another foreign Order and I am of the opinion that the Benedictines would do as well if not better than any other. And there would be the advantage that their mother house would be in the country and we could have some better control.' But he left it to Bute to decide. Meanwhile, a letter from Frigolet intimated that the canons at Wigtown and Craigeach would be withdrawn after Trinity Sunday. The bishop was not amused. 'So I must soon take steps to provide for the mission or her ladyship will again be deprived of chaplains for the school. It will give trouble every way.'[52]

In retrospect: the distance of Whithorn from the major centres of population in Scotland (admittedly, this had not worried pre-Reformation Premonstratensians in the Isles) is only less striking than its remoteness from an abbey in Provence. Clearly, the historic associations of the place, where canons of Prémontré formed the chapter of the mediaeval cathedral, had been the decisive factor in the calculation.[53] But the antiquarian enthusiasm of the Marquess, even combined with the adventurous spirit of the second abbot of Frigolet, was not enough to guarantee success. Rosemary Hannah, Bute's biographer, wrote of an earlier disappointment, this time from Benedictines of the English

51 Hannah, *The Grand Designer*, p. 276, relying on a letter of 18 October 1890 from the Bishop of Galloway to Lord Bute. Bute Archives, BU/21/274.

52 Letter of 23 January 1896 from Bishop William Turner to Lord Bute. Bute Archives, BU/21/366. 'Her Ladyship' was Gwendolen Crichton-Stuart (1854–1932).

53 Oswald Hunter Blair, 'Whithorn Priory', *Catholic Encyclopaedia* (New York: Robert Appleton, 1907–12), vol. XV, *s.v.* It might be noted that David (Oswald) Hunter Blair, fifth baronet and titular abbot of Dunfermline, was Bute's earliest biographer: *John Patrick, Third Marquess of Bute, K. T. (1847–1900). A Memoir* (London: Murray, 1921). The biography's tone was occasionally sardonic on the topic of Bute's ecclesiastical schemes, describing (for instance) as 'fantastic' Bute's plan to restore the ruins of the cathedral of St Andrews as a University church', p. 208.

Congregation, 'Bute might have been happier if he had spent more time in historical research and writing, for ecclesiastical matters often drove him to fury'.[54] One suspects that the Whithorn scheme was among them.

Evidently the diocese of Galloway did not hold the failure of this Premonstratensian project against the canons regular– or perhaps its officials had short memories. In any case, a second attempt in Dumfries and Galloway—this time in the twentieth century—would be owed not to Frigolet but to the Irish foundation from Tongerlo: Kilnacrott in Country Cavan, the 'Lakeland' (reputedly, 365 lakes in all) of the island of Ireland. Though, as just noted, this was never a Frigolet mission, it will be convenient, since it constitutes the sole remaining Scottish element in attempted Norbertine restoration in Britain, to mention it here.

In 1958 two canons from Kilnacrott were sent to assist in the parish of St Columba in Annan, a market town on the river of the same name, best known as the place of education of Thomas Carlyle.[55] In 1971, now boosted to a trio, and in pastoral charge of the place, they transferred their efforts to a very different venue, the church of Our Lady of Mount Carmel in the Onthank district of Kilmarnock, Ayrshire's largest town and the most populous burgh in the diocese. Sited in an area of multiple deprivation, it was an endeavour comparable, on a small scale, to Tongerlo's transfer of canons from Lincolnshire farmland to Miles Platting's soot and grime. Unlike Corpus Christi Manchester (or indeed, for that matter the earlier Lincolnshire houses), the Irish Norbertines made little attempt to organize the sort of conventual life one would expect from a dependent priory.[56] Unsurprisingly, Scottish vocations to the priesthood did not favour this foundling, with the splendid exception of the Glasgow-born Celtic scholar Cadoc Leighton (1950–2020), whose life, however, after entering Kilnacrott Abbey, was divided between Ireland, the United States, and Cornwall. Across the Tamar, he served as parish priest of Camborne, where he blessed his flock, often to their surprise, in the tongue of ancient Kernow. The Kilmarnock canons did, however, attract a lay brother, John Kane, a former professional soldier in the British Army, who left behind him a memory of gold.[57]

By 1999 the total of Norbertine fathers recorded as in residence by the *Catholic Directory for Scotland* had fallen from a half dozen—sign of a

54 Hannah, *The Grand Designer*, p. 130.

55 *Catholic Directory for the Clergy and Laity of Scotland, 1958* (Glasgow: John S. Burns & Sons, 1958), p. 154. I am grateful to the Revd John McLean of Ayr for drawing my attention to the Kilnacrott presence at Annan.

56 E-letter of 6 June 2023 to the author from William Fitzgerald, O.Praem., currently the administrator of the human survivors and material remains of Kilnacrott, though resident at St Michael's Abbey, Silverado, CA.

57 *Ibid.*

serious attempt at implantation—to a mere two, a number corresponding precisely to the original investment at Annan some forty years before.[58] It was, perhaps, just as well for the standing of the Order of Prémontré in Britain that the house shut its doors when it did, in 2000, and even that was perilously late. In the closing decade of the twentieth century the reputation of Kilnacrott's Abbey of the Holy Trinity was destroyed by the activities of a serial paedophile, Brendan Smyth (1927–97), a Northern Irishman from Belfast. The affair—including its attempted 'cover-up'—was sufficiently serious to bring down a coalition government in the Irish Republic, even if it (just) failed to topple from his throne an archbishop of Armagh.[59] Fifteen years later the abbey buildings were sold and the contents auctioned off, to a chorus of excoriation in both Catholic and secular circles. A disaster for the fortunes of Prémontré in Ireland, both North and South, the shadow of ill-repute did not, thankfully, extend beyond the Irish Sea.

---

58 *Catholic Directory for Scotland, 1999* (Glasgow: John S. Burns & Sons, 1999), p. 232.

59 Chris Moore, *Betrayal of Trust. The Father Brendan Smyth Affair and the Catholic Church* (Dublin: Marino, 1995).

~ 9 ~

Fortunes of History:
From Frigolet to Tongerlo

I T IS A RELIEF to return from that detour, via a late Scottish grandchild of the Flemish abbey, to the works and pomps of the Provençal refugees. With the signal exception of Storrington, their foundations do seem distinctly evanescent. Yet evaluation of the conduct of Abbot Boniface on the British mission must in all fairness take into account the emergency nature of the situation with which anti-clerical—indeed anti-Christian—administrative action of the French State confronted him. He had on his hands a diaspora of Religious in a strange land. Even so, his response was remarkably scatter-gun. It depended on the favour of exiled royalty (Eugénie), British aristocrats (Bute, Norfolk), or English gentry (the de Barys), none of whom necessarily understood the conditions in which Premonstratensian foundations might best thrive. In the case of Ambleside, implantation was the work of a Norbertine who might not unfairly be called, if the pun be forgiven, a loose cannon. In all cases, until the hand of the Administrator descended in 1893, supervision was exercised with a very light touch. In these overall circumstances, which included the forcible removal of Frigolet's second abbot and a second State-enforced expulsion from the abbey in 1903, it was hardly surprising that Tongerlo, with canons domiciled in England since the 1860s, was eventually required to pick up the pieces—or such of them as remained. That transition, Frigolet to Tongerlo, proved relatively simple to achieve owing to recent developments in the wider Catholic Church.

Pope Leo XIII did not intend to treat the definition of the universal jurisdiction of the bishop of Rome in the 1870 Conciliar decree *Pastor aeternus* as merely an ornament to his tiara. He was seriously interested in co-ordinated if not centralized organization in the Church whose supreme pastor he became in 1878. Independent groupings of Religious communities from the same traditions of monastic life—Benedictines, say, or Franciscans—offended his tidy, organizing mind. Wherever possible he sought if not to unify them then at least to link them together under figureheads who could receive and transmit papal proposals to their various constituencies. In 1893 he created the office of 'abbot primate' as a nominal head of all Benedictine Congregations of monks and nuns. In 1897 he incorporated a number of Observantine Franciscan institutes into one under the overall title *Ordo Fratrum Minorum* (though Friars Minor Capuchin and Friars Minor Conventual had perforce to be left outside). Then in 1898 he encouraged the 'Primitive Observance Congregation of France' to integrate with the main Premonstratensian Order, which in 1883 had re-established the office of abbot-general, defunct (except for a few months in 1869–70) since the time of the French Revolution. It would be the achievement at Frigolet of Denis Bonnefoy to prepare a community sharply divided on the issue of both observance and autonomy for a reconciliation with the wider Order which took place barely a year before his death. (The Latin epitaph on his tombstone at Frigolet lauds him for this signal achievement.[1])

The absorption of the Primitive Observance Congregation of France into the Order at large facilitated, if it did not ensure, the coming together of the twin tracks of Norbertine re-implantation in the British Isles. In 1935 the last French canon in England, Evermode Riot (born 1870), died at Storrington,[2] leaving as sole bearer of the Frigolet name there the unmistakably English Philip Alban Beasley-Suffolk, a product of the Warwickshire loam of Bedworth. In fact, by the 1920 testamentary arrangements of Godefroid Madelaine, abbot of Frigolet (1842–1932),[3] Beasley-Suffolk had been appointed 'executor and recipient' of the

---

1 'Here lies Brother Denis, abbot of this church, who in a time of torment was the artisan of reconciliation. With faith and goodness he revived this house with his brethren under the guidance of a single shepherd. Offering himself as a holocaust he gave himself for them.' At the dead abbot's 'month's mind' the vicar general of the diocese of Aix, after praising Abbot Boulbon who had received 'the grace of the founder', and scrupulously avoiding all mention of the second abbot, found for Abbot Bonnefoy some appropriate words of Augustine in the Matins Office for Holy Abbots. 'If you wish to raise a monumental building, apply yourself to establishing well the foundations. The higher it is to be built, the lower must they descend', 'Discours prononcé à l'issue du service de trentième jour en l'église abbatiale de Saint-Michel, par l'abbé Guillebert, vicaire générale 'd'Aix', in *Notice Biographique sur le révérendissime Père Denis, Abbé de Saint-Michel de Frigolet* (Aix: Nicot, 1899), pp. 58, 59. Frigolet Archives, Cartons Abbés, JI. 3.

2 Muston Necrology.

3 Madelaine, best known as the priest who proposed the publication of St Thérèse of Lisieux's 'Story of a Soul', was a canon of Mondaye, but his funeral oration for Denis Bonnefoy, the much-loved third abbot of Frigolet who died in his 40s, triggered his election at Frigolet in 1899: see Ardura, *L'Abbaye Saint-Michel de Frigolet*, pp. 351–6.

property at Storrington, perhaps envisaging a future of this kind. The fact that both legator and legatee were individuals reflects the lack of legal recognition of the existence of monasteries in the French law of the period—the juridical situation which made so easy the expulsion of French citizens from French soil by the Republican authorities.[4] Abbot Madelaine, a Norman and thus more attuned to the English mind-set, had promised Storrington all the help he could give it. Bernard Ardura rightly reports that during the first two decades of the century his correspondence with the priory, as held in the Frigolet Archives, is not less than 'abundant'.[5] But with his resignation as abbot in 1919 that period of epistolary productivity—and the care it betokened for the English mission—came to an end.

By that date there was in any case only Storrington left to worry about. Even at the time when Madelaine began his abbacy, the former priory at Farnborough was securely in the possession of the Solesmes Congregation, and its out-stations assigned to seculars (Bracknell) or Salesians (Farnborough town). The Frigolet missions in Whithorn, Wigtown and nearby hamlets had ended in 1898, and Ambleside—under the historically resonant name of 'Shap Cell'—was abandoned in the same year (even if, technically speaking, as a house of the Primitive Observance of France, it had already suffered suppression in 1895). Bedworth—without Weston, relinquished in 1889, though the gifted de Bary land was retained,[6] lasted somewhat longer but was abandoned before the outbreak of the Great War of 1914–18.[7] Bernard Ardura was inclined to ascribe the demise of these relatively short-lived implantations to the incompetence of Abbot Boniface. 'The numerous ephemeral foundations undertaken during this abbacy ill conceal an incoherent

---

4 *Last Will and Testament*, 24 June 1929, of Godefroid Madelaine, signed at Mesnil-Saint-Denis and witnessed in French. Muston Archives. On the background, see J.-P. Durand, *La Liberté des congrégations religieuses en France. Régimes français des congrégations religieuses* (Paris: Cerf, 1999). In recent years the last abbot of Frigolet (who returned to his own Belgian abbey of Averbode, leaving as successor in Provence a simple prior), wrote to Fra François-Marie Pourcelet to say he had visited Beasley-Murray's 'poor grave' at Storrington, a pious visit to the last Frigolet canon in England, E-letter of 12 March 2019 Thomas-Gilbert Secuianu, O.Praem., to Fra François-Marie Pourcelet, Frigolet Archives, Cartons Storrington, E31.

5 Ardura, *L'Abbaye Saint-Michel de Frigolet*, p. 92, footnote 30.

6 *Rapport sur nos maisons d'Angleterre, 1895*, p. 23. Frigolet Archives, Cartons Storrington, E29, p. 23. In his report, Xavier de Fourvière, argued for the recreation of a fledgling community precisely at Weston. 'The future of our Congregation in England is there, in this country of the Midland [*sic*], or middle earth, one of the best situated places'.

7 Ardura, *L'Abbaye Saint-Michel de Frigolet*, p. 52. In fact it was returned to the diocese of Birmingham in 1912.

administration',[8] though, to be sure, the dragoon-enforced expulsion of the canons of Frigolet hardly permitted a 'business as usual' approach.

It is not hard to discover the source for Ardura's strictures. In 1895 Xavier de Fourvière Rieux wrote a substantial report for Denis Bonnefoy, the new administrator at Frigolet. It has been drawn on several times in this account and deserves now a formal introduction to readers. Consisting of some seventy-five pages, inclusive of résumé and conclusions, this notably professional piece of analysis was followed by some brief and unsatisfactory pages of 'testimony' by the deposed abbot, Paulin Boniface, to the character of his British or at least British-based subjects. Written too late in the day for Farnborough, its remit embraced Storrington, Bedworth/Weston, and Ambleside, together with the surviving Scottish presence at Wigtown and Craigeach.

Xavier de Fourvière Rieux gave six reasons for the disappointing results hitherto achieved. They were, in the order he gave them: firstly, over-emphasis on the canonico-monastic life when, truth to tell, England was hardly ripe for monasteries of any kind as distinct from 'missions'; secondly, the lack of a geographically central position for the principal house; thirdly, the failure to acquire a solid economic basis since founders gave land but not endowments; fourthly, poor administrative practice in regard to 'personnel'—a portmanteau term that covered inadequate discernment in accepting candidates, deficiencies in their training, inept choice of individuals unsuited to particular missions (notably living and working in Protestant England), and over-frequent change of local superiors; fifthly, an insufficient unity of spirit partly explicable by the fact that some Religious had been formed according to the Primitive Constitutions, others in terms of the 'new statutes', a state of affairs compounded by the excessive latitude accorded to individual initiative; sixthly (and lastly), the high incidence of imprudent brothers who had a habit of sharing with outsiders the inside story of difficulties in the English or Scottish houses, thus besmirching the good name of the Order, particularly among bishops. Naturally enough, the fall of Abbot Boniface—the fact of which could hardly be denied even if a veil covered the aetiology—did not, in this respect, help at all.[9]

Neither *rapporteur* nor abbatial recipient could have guessed they had less than a decade in which to repair matters before a second expulsion befell Frigolet, the work (once again) of anti-clerical leadership in the Third French Republic.[10] In the wake of the new trauma of 1903, with

---

8 *Ibid.*

9 *Rapport sur nos maisons d'Angleterre, 1895*, pp. 5–9. Frigolet Archives, Cartons Storrington, E29.

10 Ardura, *Au cœur de la Provence*, pp. 100–7.

abbot and canons transferred to a Belgian redoubt at Leffe, near Dinant, conventual numbers fell. A courageous mission in Madagascar, in the vicariate-apostolic of Diego-Suarez (now Antsiranana), commenced just before the second expulsion, and despite the shrinking of the community, lasted until 1919 (and it would be resumed, once Frigolet was recovered, in the vicariate-apostolic of Antananarivo, the Malagasy capital, until 1935). Numbers never again rivalled what seems in retrospect the Provençal abbey's late-nineteenth-century springtime—though, admittedly, many members of the Frigolet community of that epoch were not actually priests: they were, rather, *frères convers*, tertiaries, and oblates.

Nor did the eventual return to French soil guarantee expansion. In 1930 the sixth abbot of Frigolet, Léon Perrier (1881–1948), attending a General Chapter at the Louvain abbey of Parc, would go to the trouble of crossing the Channel to visit Storrington but could only lament the shortage of Religious to re-staff Frigolet's prize dependency to the degree desirable.[11] And after the defeat of France in 1940 it was scarcely feasible for war-time Frigolet to send anyone, notwithstanding the fact that the abbey was situated outside German-occupied France, in the Vichy zone.

In 1946, however, a period of modest yet real revival began which, in the years before the Second Vatican Council, would make of Frigolet an exemplary, if not numerically huge, Premonstratensian abbey, and, in the favourably prejudiced opinion of one historian, something of a 'pastoral model for the twentieth century'.[12] Suddenly well-known in France thanks to television and radio coverage of its liturgy (new media which, so far as Religious communities were concerned, it pioneered), and with a widely distributed book-length celebration of its life and work (prefaced by an Academician),[13] the abbey of Saint-Michel de Frigolet embarked upon a fresh epoch. That in turn was sealed by the election of its seventh abbot Norbert Calmels (1908–85) as abbot-general of the entire Order in 1962.[14] But by then Storrington was in other Norbertine hands, and the Frigolet connexion disappears from this story.

One episode in the narrative has not yet been mentioned, save in passing. In 1893 the founding abbot of the post-Storrington English and Scottish ventures had been—rather spectacularly—relieved of his

11 Ardura, *L'Abbaye Saint-Michel de Frigolet*, p. 103.

12 *Ibid.*, pp. 107–20.

13 R. Serrou—P. Vals, *Les Prémontrés. Chez les Pères Blancs de Frigolet*, Préface de *Marcel Pagnol, de l'Académie française* (Paris: Pierre Horay, 1958).

14 Ardura, *L'Abbaye Saint-Michel de Frigolet*, pp. 375–89. By the second decade of the twenty-first century the 'renaissance' at Frigolet had spent itself, to the extent that in 2015 an effectively empty abbey had to be re-colonized from Sant' Antimo, outside Siena, a 'wild' community of reformed Premonstratensians founded by a former canon of Mondaye, André Michel Forest (1931–2022).

charge by the Holy See and reduced to the lay state. The 'incompetence' alleged by Ardura had consisted, in the latter's eyes, not so much in failure to maintain these far-flung commitments of the Frigolet diaspora as in the folly of making the commitments in the first place. Yet the real problem with Paulin Boniface, in the eyes of Rome, was not over-optimistic monastic dispersion. It fell under a very different heading: 'Cherchez la femme', though money was also involved. The archbishop of Aix, named 'apostolic visitor of the Prémontrés of the Congregation of France' wrote from Frigolet to all members of the community. 'We have made a scrupulously detailed canonical enquiry and have sent the dossier to Rome. Father Paulinus has spent several weeks there in order to explain and defend himself: the result has been a condemnation much more severe than mine. He stubbornly resists the orders of the Sovereign Pontiff and my own; in particular he refused to return the monies of the Abbey which he holds onto unjustly.'[15] Reduced to the lay state, the second abbot of Frigolet would die at Avignon, in close proximity, therefore, to the abbey whose choir-school, an inspired work of the founding prior, he had entered as a boy. It was as well that his five successor abbots, spanning the period between 1899 and the opening of the Second Vatican Council, were of a different stamp—which is simply to say that, at the very least, they did not suffer shipwreck.[16]

What, then, of the fate of Storrington itself, the prize possession in the Frigolet diaspora? Xavier de Fourvière Rieux's 1895 report had not been favourable to Storrington's primacy among the surviving Frigolet houses—or even, indeed, to its continuance. But, in the opinion of its author, if it were to be retained as the principal house, then a novitiate, fleetingly established in Storrington's earliest years, would need to be re-created. Now, however, it would not be a novitiate in exile, since Frigolet, in the mid-1890s, had a thriving novitiate on its own soil. It

15 Letter of 27 January 1894 from Archbishop François-Xavier Gouthe-Soulard (1819–1900) of Aix to the Reverend Fathers and Very Dear Brethren [of Frigolet]', Frigolet Archives, Cartons Storrington, E31.

16 In point of fact, at least three of the later abbots (the fifth, sixth, and seventh abbots) have been the subjects of admiring biographies: Romain Vedel, *Un homme de Dieu, le Réverendissime Päère Adrien Borelly, abbé de Saint-Michel de Frigolet, 1838–1931* (Avignon: Aubanel, 1932)'; H. Monnier, *Le Rèverendissime Père Léon Perrier, abbé de Saint-Michel de Frigolet, 1881–1948* (Frigolet: Abbaye Saint-Michael de Frigolet, 1948); Claude Durix, *Norbert Calmels. Histoire d'une amitié, 1944–1985* (Paris: Guy Trédaniel, 1986). In 1978 Pope Paul VI made Abbot Calmels titular bishop of Dusa and Pro-Nuncio in Morocco, as well as his personal representative to King Hassan II: Ardua, *Au cœur de la Provence*, p. 113. He was also a candidate for election to the Académie Française (information provided by Fra François-Marie Pourcelet in a conversation of 3 October 2023).

would be a specifically English novitiate. And where, he asked, might a suitable English novice-master be found?

This cool—not to say glacial—appraisal was not universally shared. On the eve of the First World War Abbot Madelaine went to Storrington, and his visitation report was positively glowing. The sometime adviser to St Thérèse (1873–97) found in the Sussex priory 'a spirit of union and charity and a great good will to assure the future of the mission', prospects for which looked distinctly rosy under a 'wise administrator' in the shape of a new prior, François Laborde.[17] Yet after the Great War, when the Frigolet community, temporarily housed in Belgium, suffered fresh indignities at the hands of the Imperial German Army,[18] the general if slow Inter-War decline, already noted, could hardly leave Storrington unscathed. The sheer number of Abbot Madelaine's letters to Storrington, as held in the Frigolet Archives, interspersed with those of other writers but chronologically arranged for the period of his abbacy (1899–1919), testifies to his concern.[19] But the toll of events brought about his premature resignation. Signing himself *abbas cedens* he explained what anyone might have guessed. 'There was first of all the dissolution of the Religious Orders which in 1903 obliged us to quit our dear France and to reconstitute ourselves far from *la patrie*. Then in 1914 came the War, the great testing. Here [at Leffe] it was terribly hard for us all, the existence of the Abbey was at stake ... All that a father can suffer in the midst of these storms! But it is useless to recall it now.'[20] His withdrawal was a blow for Storrington, for which he had shown particular solicitude. But the volume of letters of petition and thanks from the 'simple faithful' retained in the Frigolet Archives, suggests a wide response to the devotional exercises—notably, in the novena form—arranged by the community, with accompanying donations which assisted viability.

Under his successor, Adrien Borelly (1852–1928), abbot from 1920 to 1928, decline seemed inevitable, with the Sussex house reduced at times to a quartet of members. As early as 1923 Philip Beasley-Suffolk is found writing to Abbot Borelly with the alarming report that duties within the priory, falling disproportionately as they did on the prior and himself,

---

17 Visitation Report, 24 April 1913. Frigolet Archives, Cartons Storrington, E29.
18 'Indignities': the abbey was turned into a prison for 1800 women convicts. One Norbertine priest and a laybrother were shot. Seventeen canons, including the abbot, were dispatched to Germany as prisoners of war, but on reaching Luxemburg were released on parole and found refuge with the Benedictines of Chevetogne. Of the sixty canons who had left Frigolet in 1903, only thirty remained at Leffe by 1919: thus Ardura, *Au cœur de la Provence*, p. 107.
19 Frigolet Archives, Cartons Storrington, E31.
20 Letter of 14 November 1919 from Abbot Godefroid Madelaine to 'My very dear confreres'. Frigolet Archives, Cartons Storrington, E31.

had reached the point where not only pastoral work outside the house but even the most elementary recreational requirements of healthy living seemed out of the question. 'There are months and months where I have not been out of the monastery even to take a walk.'[21] Prior Laborde wrote to the abbot in 1926: 'The [First World] War and the ruinous taxes have made our task extremely difficult and slow', noting with some envy that 'the Belgian Premonstratensians [i. e. the canons of Tongerlo] have opened a novitiate in Ireland [at Kilnacrott]', thus stealing a march on Storrington which had as yet no equivalent, tailor-made for the English.[22] But in a letter of the following year the same writer noted how 'at this moment there is a great movement of return to Catholicism in England', such that 'the future [meaning, presumably, for Storrington, or at least the White Canons in Britain] seems full of hope'.[23]

In 1930 Borelly's successor, the recently elected Abbot Léon Perrier, who would preside at Frigolet until almost the end of 'French' Storrington (he retired as abbot in 1946), instituted Philip Beasley-Suffolk as 'residential prior', in a letter full of personal praise for his qualities but also marked by foreboding at how he might be able to exhibit them.[24] In a decade the fifty-year old English canon would be dead. And no one was left to step into his shoes.

After 1939, with France's declaration of war against Hitlerite Germany, the priory of Storrington fell empty. Any surviving Religious of military age and French nationality was obliged to serve the Republic in its hour of need. As an anonymous Norbertine, writing in the *Catholic Gazette*, noted by way of retrospect on Storrington's history, the programme of conscription constituted a 'strange reversion of things': the same Third Republic that had (twice) expelled the canons of Frigolet now required them, *volens nolens*, to return to France.[25] After requisitioning by the British military authorities during the 'Phoney War', the Storrington premises were commandeered by the Seventh Infantry Brigade of the Canadian army. Some damage was done, partly through neglect (thus woodworm used the opportunity to eat through the original choirstalls). The shape of things to come was announced when in 1942 a Mancunian

21 Letter of 29 January 1923 from Philip Beasley-Suffolk, O.Praem., to Abbot Adrien Borelly. Frigolet Archives, Cartons Storrington, E28.

22 Letter of 6 July 1926 from François Laborde, O.Praem., to Abbot Adrien Borelly. Frigolet Archives, Cartons Storrington, E 28.

23 Letter of 30 December 1927 from the Prior of Storrington to Abbot Adrien Borelly. Frigolet Archives, Cartons Storrington, E 28.

24 Letter of 22 August 1930 from Abbot Léon Perrier to Philip Beasley-Suffolk, O.Praem. Frigolet Archives, Cartons Storrington, E 28.

25 C. R. P., 'The Shrine of Our Lady of England', *Catholic Gazette*, 48/5 (May 1957), pp. 106–7, and here at p. 106.

canon of Tongerlo, Edward Dodds (1895–1962), became priest in charge of the parish, the monastery itself being presumably out of bounds since it was now a military installation.[26]

But a 'transitus' of the house from Frigolet to Tongerlo was not by any means a done deal. Three years and more after the War's ending, Anselm Cross, writing from Manchester in his capacity as Rector or 'General Superior' of the (Tongerlo) English Mission, proposed to Abbot Stalmans that in the event of Frigolet resuming control of Storrington — as was bruited abroad — such a move would at least have the desirable effect of releasing manpower sorely needed by himself when wearing his other hat as prior of Corpus Christi, Miles Platting.[27] But Frigolet's second thoughts came to nothing. In 1952 Tongerlo, under the same abbot, accepted formal responsibility for Storrington, which, despite its relatively modest scale, was the largest and best appointed of Norbertine conventual buildings in England.

As a hard-headed Fleming, Stalmans had not appropriated Storrington for Tongerlo without first gaining adequate knowledge of some relevant facts. Sunday Mass attendance was estimated at 160 persons, with, however, few children among them. The congregation was predominantly female and elderly. Many of the adults present were converts about the quality of whose instruction in the faith some question was raised.[28] Materially, there was need for a proper heating system, and the extension of electrical light from the church and cloister to the remaining rooms whence, mysteriously, all furniture had disappeared, with the presumption that it had either been sold or had been shipped back to Frigolet.[29] These reports, on, respectively, matters pastoral and financial, were received in the autumn of 1946. Not till five years later did a surveyor's findings note that, taking into account the costs of refurbishment, the value of the property in its present condition stood at around fifty thousand pounds.[30]

It was not, then, a paltry house nor was the land it included a negligi-

---

26 For a list of the priors and parish priests of Storrington, see the appendices in Simon Mole, *Catholic Life in Storrington. The Comings and Goings since 1880* (no place, no publisher, 2022).

27 Letter of 15 February 1949 from Anselm Cross, O.Praem., to Abbot Stalmans of Tongerlo. Tongerlo Archives, E2 Engeland en Storrington, Box 5, 33. Two canons of Tongerlo were at Storrington as of this date.

28 Letter of 21 September 1946 from Cuthbert Ryan, O.Praem., to Abbot Stalmans. Tongerlo Archives, E2 Storrington en Engeland, Box 5, 40.

29 Letter of 30 September 1946 from Felim Colwell, O.Praem., to Abbot Stalmans, Tongerlo Archives, E2 Storrington en Engeland, Box 5, 40.

30 'The Monastery, Storrington', by John C. Allwork, Surveyor, Land Agent and Valuer, 17 October 1951. Tongerlo Archives, E2 Storrington en Engeland, Box 5, 40.

ble quantity. The vista was enticing. The aim was to make it the Order's main house in England and the novitiate house for future growth. It had long been a concern for the Tongerlo canons both in Lincolnshire and at Manchester that any youthful vocations coming their way were necessarily dispatched to the mother-abbey for their training—with the attendant disadvantages (not least, in Flanders, linguistic) of expatriation. An undated letter from Matthew Smith to Abbot Hugo Lamy (1879–1949) of Tongerlo, (before 1937 when Lamy demitted office), had raised the question of insular formation. Admittedly, 'Storrington is not ours at Tongerlo', but would its dependence on Frigolet necessarily mean it could not become 'the [common] novitiate for England', including those whose obedience was to the Belgian abbey, rather than the French?[31] In the changed canonical situation that was now in prospect, that aporia no longer existed. In February 1952 Abbot Stalmans wrote to Dodds' fellow canon, Cuthbert Ryan (1882–1965), parish priest of Storrington from 1947 until that year, authorizing him to offer the abbot and canons of Frigolet the sum of 11, 000 francs (or 10, 000 in the event of their finding a lower figure acceptable).[32] Frigolet had never been wealthy. The deal went through. The Frigolet Archives retain the deed in English and in French: it was no doubt correct in English law, but its grasp of the canonical situation of the two Abbeys left something to be desired.[33]

On 3 July 1952 the Norbertine abbot-general confirmed the erection of a novitiate at Storrington. On 21 August 1952, the priory was officially re-opened, and the following day a High Mass was celebrated by Abbot Stalmans in the presence of the local bishop.[34] It was a new and encouraging start in an era—the pontificate of Pius XII (1876–1958) who became pope in 1939—marked by considerable corporate confidence in the Roman Catholic Church. That is so even if certain strains were already apparent beneath the generally tranquil and assured surface.

A Christmastide 1953 letter to 'Friends' of Storrington from the prior, Felim Colwell (1914–68), was extraordinarily confident. Colwell reported that restoration was almost complete for a community of 'at least thirty'. (The east side of the cloister constituted the principal con-

31 Undated letter of Matthew Smith, O.Praem., to Abbot Lamy, Tongerlo Archives, E2 Engeland en Storrington, Box 4, 27. Smith's other suggestions were that postulants should go to Kilnacrott and students, following the noviciate, to Crowle.

32 Letter of 28 February 1952 from Abbot Stalmans to Thomas Cuthbert Ryan, O.Praem. Muston Archives.

33 The 'Agreement'/'Accord' speaks of a contract between Abbot Norbert Calmels 'on behalf of the French Province [*sic*] of the Order of the Canons Regular of Prémontré' and Abbot Emiel Stalmans 'on behalf of the English Houses of the said Order'. Frigolet Archives, Cartons Storrington, E30.

34 C. R. P., 'The Shrine of Our Lady of England', p. 106.

ventual building; a wing on the south side, connecting the west wing with the priory church, was a later construction for the purpose of guest accommodation—it included, appropriately, the principal entrance to the complex.[35]) Indeed, said Prior Colwell, the majority of rooms were already occupied, and he looked forward to the house becoming a full abbey of the Order.[36] Up Kithurst Lane, the Dominican Sisters of the Bushey Congregation (the 'Dominican Sisters of St Catherine of Siena of Newcastle, Natal') were opening a Catholic (but fee-paying) school. 'The Abbey', acquired from the Ravenscroft family, was bought for them, for this purpose, by the canons.[37] And, continued Colwell, it was hoped in the near future to establish close by the priory a juniorate for boys.

The equivalent of a minor seminary (compare the 'juvénat' of Frigolet, perhaps reflected in the 'Home School' ventures at Ambleside and Wigtown as well as the 'boarding school' at Spalding), this would shortly eventuate on Greyfriars Lane, Storrington, under the title 'St Norbert's College', and was provided with an elaborate code for organization and discipline.[38] The College had the good fortune to be housed in Gerston House (re-christened by Colwell's successor, Joseph Gerebern Neill (1911–76), 'St Joseph's Hall'). Built between 1908 and 1910 in the 'Vernacular Revival' style—here represented in the form of Sussex flint—almost certainly by Edward Schroeder Prior (1852–1932), for an American businessman,[39] the house was furnished in the Arts and Crafts manner represented locally by the ever-memorable Guild community of St Joseph and St Dominic on nearby Ditchling Common.[40]

35 Information provided by Martin Gosling, O.Praem., in a conversation of 13 June 2023.

36 Prior's Letter of Christmas 1953. Muston Archives.

37 Information provided by Martin Gosling, O.Praem., in a conversation of 13 June 2023. The school continued into the late 1990s, after which—but still under its 'monastic' name, 'St Joseph's Abbey'—it became a private dwelling.

38 Tongerlo Archives, E2 Engeland en Storrington, Box 5, 43. Storrington was in possession of a copy of the charter of the Frigolet school, *Juvénat des RR. PP. Prémontrés de la Congregation de France*, with an account of the school's aims, organization, and admission requirements. It belongs with a number of documents transferred from Muston to Frigolet by Thomas Swaffer, O.Praem., in September 2019. Now in Frigolet Archives, Cartons Storrington, E34.

39 On which figure see M. G. Cook, *Edward Prior: Arts and Crafts Architect* (Marlborough: Crowood Press, 2015).

40 Timothy Wilcox (ed.), *Eric Gill and the Guild of St Joseph and St Dominic* (Hove: Hove Museum and Art Gallery, 1990); see more widely, Mary Greensted, *The Arts and Crafts Movement in Britain* (Oxford: Shire, 2010). The Hall, which, in an exercise of emergency charity, doubled up as a home for refugees in the twenty-four months following the Hungarian Uprising of 1956, was relinquished for a remarkably low sum to David John Cashman (1912–71), the first bishop of the new diocese of

Furthermore, thirty-five acres of new land had been acquired and in 1954 a large outdoors statue was to be erected opposite the canons' church in an obvious attempt to enhance the priory's visibility. 'Backed by the rising ground with its Grotto-like appearance Our Lady's statue looks over lawns sprinkled with modest saplings and simple blooms, presenting a vision of peace and blessedness both to the pilgrims who come to pray before it and to the friendly non-Catholics who pause to gaze at it as they pass along.'[41] (The outdoor statue survives, not in its original position, but in Matt's Wood, a higher piece of land to the east of the priory grounds.) In the Marian year Pius XII had just proclaimed there was, thought Colwell, a perfectly reasonable hope for expansion in the number of pilgrims to 'Our Lady of England'.

Though Colwell's priorship was cut short by his election as the first abbot of Kilnacrott (he was from Dromore, in County Down), Storrington showed every sign of developing according to his vision in the years immediately preceding the Second Vatican Council. In 1954 the following signed their petitions for 'transitus' from the Abbey of Onze Lieve Vrouw at Tongerlo to the 'house of Storrington': Kevin Cassidy, Anselm Cross, Edward Dodds, Norbert Ellis, Aloysius Firth, Idesbald Joye, Oliver Kelly, Patrick Kerigan, Hubert Mathee, George Mulligan, Gerebern Neill, Cuthbert Ryan, John Baptist Turner. In 1955 a new abbot at Tongerlo, Joost Marcel Boel (1919–2006), was able to write to a new prior at Storrington, Hubert Mathee (1919–96), a native of Holland (the Dutch original, not its Lincolnshire derivative), that a possible postulant for the equally new Storrington novitiate, was already on the horizon.[42]

In May 1955 Abbot Boel came in person to conduct a visitation, accompanied by the claustral prior from Tongerlo. In the upshot he chose to delay any kind of visitation instructions since (as he explained) he wished to confer at length with the abbot-general, with Felim Colwell at Kilnacrott, neo-abbot and former very successful prior of Storrington, and, finally, with Anselm Cross who was to remain 'Regular Superior' of the Order in England. This appears to have created a certain vacuum. To judge by his correspondence with Tongerlo, Prior Mathee was not a decisive man. Letters about personalities, money, and the use of property were sent almost weekly to Abbot Boel during his priorship, to be answered, in some cases, three or four at a time. The abbot came again in January 1958, and, no doubt wisely, left on departure a missive

Arundel and Brighton, on its creation in 1965. The diocese sold it at the behest of the fourth bishop, Kieran Conry (born 1951), in 2004.

41 C. R. P., 'The Shrine of Our Lady of England', p. 107.

42 Letter of 12 September 1955 from Abbot Marcel Boel to Hubert Mathee, O.Praem. Tongerlo Archives, E2 Engeland en Storrington, Box 5, 48/1.

that was certainly direct. The thistle of personal friction was firmly grasped—at any rate in an epoch when monastic imprisonment was no longer a possibility. 'Let us, in a spirit of Christian charity, try to see and appreciate the good in each other. And in the same spirit of charity, let us try to bear each others' shortcomings and weaknesses nobly'. Applying that highly general lesson to the specificities of Storrington, Abbot Boel noted how 'it is not possible in a small community to define all authorities with exactitude and to foresee all works and duties in their smallest details'. The issue of nationality was also clearly tackled. 'In order that the Norbertine religious foundation in England may be in reality an English foundation, those confreres who are not English will take care especially that, in a spirit of continuous self-denial, they make the English mentality, conceptions and customs, which are not in strife with religious observance, their own'.[43] At the same time, patience was asked of the English, particularly with the language-problems encountered by Flemish lay-brothers. The horary, and monastic observance generally, were spelled out in plain though perfectly reasonable terms. And the abbot addressed a grey area which had obviously been giving new recruits some heartache if not headache. 'For the efficient and regular furthering of Ecclesiastical studies, a favourable solution will be studied and put into effect.'[44]

In the years remaining before the Second Vatican Council this promise seems not to have been achieved. Though an Ordination programme was assembled, and the modest priory library sufficed for the preparation of basic courses, none of the professors held any formal qualification in either theology or philosophy. While it was thought unlikely that the Order's Commission for Studies would consider the situation permanently tenable, to send the students elsewhere would be to lose their services in providing the daily Sung Office and Missa Cantata which were the glory of the renewed house. The only satisfactory solution was a remote one: namely, to hope that, over time, sufficient men would be sent for higher studies to staff a studium, acceptably equipped, in Storrington itself.

These difficulties were, however, a matter of esoteric knowledge. To post-War English Catholics at large, Storrington was becoming well-known and respected. It was a popular venue for the 'Dowry of Mary' pilgrimages sponsored by the Catholic Truth Society at a period of steady Catholic growth in England, a time which was also, in the wider Church, a high point in the corporate expression of Marian piety. In 1959,

43 Letter of 28 January 1958 from Abbot Marcel Boel to the Prior and Confraters of Storrington, Tongerlo Archives, E2 Engeland en Storrington, Box 5, 49.
44 *Ibid.*

the fiftieth anniversary of its building, the priory church of 'Our Lady of England' was consecrated, and the statue of devotion (in the church, not the outside statue) crowned, by Cyril Cowderoy (1905–76), the seventh bishop (later the first archbishop) of Southwark. With excellent taste, consecration crosses were commissioned from the sculptor Joseph Cribb at the Guild of St Joseph and St Dominic. (Cribb sent in his bill on 5 June of that year for 'crosses carved and painted, edges gilded'.[45]) One Melchior Sinkins, describing himself as 'Catholic Adviser' to the 'Overseas Press Division' of the British Government's 'Central Office of Information' on Westminster Bridge Road (founded in 1946 as successor to the wartime Ministry of Information), wrote to the then parish priest of Storrington, Kevin Cassidy (1914–2003), offering his services—presumably gratis—as press officer for the occasion. 'I first developed a deep affection for you all at Storrington when seven years ago ... we made the Priory the first stop on the first never-to-be-forgotten Round Britain Pilgrimage to the Shrines of Our Lady organized by the C. T. S [Catholic Truth Society].'[46]

Kevin Cassidy, an Irishman 'much devoted to Our Blessed Lady', was not without his own skills as a publicist.[47] He sent John XXIII (1881–1963) the wooden rosary that 'for more than fifty years has been in the hands of Our Lady of England', asking for it to be blessed by the Pope—and, obviously, returned in due course to Storrington. 'It is', wrote Cassidy, 'our fervent hope and prayer that Our Lady of England will accept our humble gift [of the statue's crowning] as an act of love and reparation for all the outrages and insults inflicted on her maternal heart since the time when our unhappy land separated itself from unity with Christ's Vicar'.[48]

As to the crowning itself, a local newspaper at Horsham reported in advance of the event, which fell on 20 June, that the bishop of Southwark 'will place two crowns, fashioned and made from diamonds, pearls, other jewels, gold and silver given by the village people on the heads of the Blessed Virgin and of the Divine Infant cradled in her left arm'—wording which suggests a degree of plagiarization from the priory's own announcement, though the jewels were donated from all over England (and indeed, in a gracious gesture though perhaps also

45 Invoice of 5 June 1959 from Joseph Cribb to 'St Mary's Priory, Storrington'. Muston Archives.

46 Letter of 15 April 1959 from Melchior A. A. Sinkins, TOSF, to Kevin Cassidy, O.Praem. Muston Archives.

47 The phrase comes from the obit notice in the Muston Necrology.

48 Letter of 13 May 1959 from Kevin Cassidy, O.Praem., to Pope John XXIII. Muston Archives.

an ironic one, from Ireland).[49] A much fuller account was offered subsequently by *Brabants Nieuwsblad* whose reporter emphasized the 'deep impression' made on Anglicans by the procession and the ceremonial event.[50] From a Low Countries perspective, it was piquant to juxtapose the Dutch prior, from Zevenbergen (near Breda, in North Brabant), with the exotically Anglian 'Onze Lieve Vrouw van Engeland'.

No trouble had been spared, so the *Catholic Guardian* assured its readers. 'Fifteen convents combined to present tableaux of the rosary; others depicted some famous shrines of Our Lady; Catholic organizations of all kinds were represented; nuns of various Orders walked together and for the first time since the Reformation members of the Third Order of St Norbert followed their banner through English lanes. The Irish and Belgian ambassadors were present in person, while the Dutch ambassador was officially represented.'[51] Local Members of Parliament attended, though Bernard Norfolk was away from Arundel Castle.

Access to the jubilee events was not so easy since the railway line (from Victoria Station) ran only to Pulborough, after which transport by bus was needed. But not only was it a well-attended event, with some (estimated) five thousand pilgrims travelling to Storrington that day, often by specially chartered coaches. It was also a widely reported one, though not, curiously, by the largest circulation religious paper in Britain, *The Universe and Catholic Times*. Prior Mathee lamented the omission in letters to the editor a week later: 'Where dozens of secular papers, both daily and weekly publications, have given the Solemn Crowning of the Statue of Our Lady of England every attention, and even BBC and ITV, and Press and Radio abroad to an unusual extent, the biggest Catholic paper has ignored the whole thing'.[52] He ended by expressing regret that the thrice yearly paid advertisements he had inserted in the paper had been so little heeded by its own management.

More widely, the house thrived sufficiently to become an independent priory in 1962, with Joseph Gerebern Neill its first prior *de regimine*. Archbishop Cyril Cowderoy of Southwark, responding to Abbot Boel's request for a formal approbation, wrote affirmatively: 'I very willingly give my approbation for the erection of a "prioratus sui juris" at Storring-

49 'Catholic Priory Celebrates Golden Jubilee', presumably from the *West Sussex County Times* (the only Horsham based newspaper). Muston Archives.

50 'Katholieke triomfdag in zonovergoten Storrington', *Brabants Nieuwsblad*, 22 June 1959, p. 3. Muston Archives.

51 'Jubilee Celebrations at Storrington', *Catholic Guardian*, 26 June 1959, p. 2. Muston Archives. In quite what sense Norbertine tertiaries existed in pre-Reformation England is perhaps a moot point.

52 Letter of 29 June 1959 from Prior Mathee to the Editor, *The Universe/The Catholic Times*. Muston Archives.

ton, to be elevated at opportune time to the state of "abbatia sui juris"'.[53] That change in status did not, naturally enough, solve all problems, but at first vocations were good. In 1961, the year that preceded the Second Vatican Council, Prior Neill was able to tell the abbot of Tongerlo that the community had swelled to the number of thirty-three. 'We can now count seven priests, seven novices, three professed brothers, three lay-brothers and one postulant brother, and twelve boys at the college'—the latter included since, *ceteris paribus*, it was expected they would go on to enter the Order.[54] In August 1962 Abbot Boel, along with a canon of Berne Abbey in the Netherlands made one final last visitation—but now this was not in his own name as abbot of Tongerlo but in that rather of the abbot-general of the entire Order.[55]

Just under a decade later, Prior Neill resigned on 16 January 1971, worn down (on his own account in correspondence with Abbot Boel—who remained the 'founding abbot' of Storrington, and thus enjoyed a certain moral authority there) by waves of criticism. It was not easy to be a Religious superior in the immediately Post-Conciliar age in the Catholic Church. He left behind a group numerically diminished when compared with its high-point of ten years previously, though one whose finances he had greatly improved, not least through the opening of a printer's. Declining the opportunity to share in the deliberations about a successor, he moved to Manchester as parish priest of Corpus Christi, thus unwittingly anticipating a possible division of the canonry (into two halves: Storrington and Manchester) which became a reality in years to come.

George Idesbald Joye (1919–98), born in Zeebrugge, succeeded him as the second prior *de regimine*, remaining in office for a substantial period from 1971 to 1986. Thinking back, it may be, to Abbot Boel's adjurations to give primacy to the English, he began his priorship by applying for British nationality. His other initiatives were not so successful. Planning to build on the economic undertakings of his predecessor, he opened a veal farm—but this was at a time when animal rights protests in the United Kingdom were just beginning, and it had to be shut down. He constructed a rather rudimentary parish hall to the north side of the priory cloister—useful enough for parishioners but not a life-changing development for the community of canons. In the wake of the post-Con-

53 Letter of 15 June 1954 from Archbishop Cyril Cowderoy to Abbot Marcel Boel, Box 6, 54.

54 Letter of 10 January 1961 from Prior Neill to Abbot Marcel Boel. Tongerlo Archives, E2 Engeland en Storrington, Box 5, 44.

55 'Results of the visitation made from August 18 to August 22, 1962, on behalf of the abbot-general in St Mary's Priory, Storrington', Box 6, 57.

ciliar disequilibrium, vocations were few and far between. The wider setting of Storrington in the English Norbertine landscape became a matter
of controversy of its own. The distance between the entities of the Order,
and between its parishes, was a problem to which, in 1981, attention was
drawn by visitators, an abbot of the Dutch abbey of Berne accompanied
by a canon of Tongerlo. They received from the confraters comments to
the effect that a greater concentration was needed in the North (at that
point: Manchester, along with the Lincolnshire and Yorkshire houses
or parishes) while in the South the future of Storrington itself, as an
independent canonry, could hardly be termed secure.[56] Prudently, the
visitors suggested deferring to a General Chapter a proposal to make
Storrington an abbey in the following year, 1982, which would both
mark the centenary of its foundation from Frigolet and honour the first
visit to England of a reigning pope. That was, of course, St John Paul II.

The reserved response was justified. At a meeting of the Canonry
Chapter in April 1982, discussion of the question whether Storrington
should continue to be 'the centre' produced an exactly split vote.[57] The
advent of a determined and traditional-minded successor to Prior Joye,
Michael Gallagher (already encountered in Chapter 4 above), as the
third prior *de regimine* from 1986 to 1992, could do nothing in the short
term to change all that.

What degree of continuity with the Abbey life of Tongerlo, with its
elaborate liturgy and robust tradition of monastic observance, was
necessary for the self-identity of English Norbertines whose own life,
limited by small numbers as it was, unfolded in a pastoral, and more
specifically parochial, context? The question mirrored, in a microcos-
mic way, the larger question facing Post-Conciliar Catholicism. What
degree of continuity with previous traditions of faith and practice,
believing and belonging, was needful for a healthy sense of continuing identity in the Church at large? At a quite different level—but one
dear to historians—the correspondence, already mentioned, between
post-War Storrington and the War-time commanding officer at the then
requisitioned priory (as well as with major-generals at the Ministry of
Defence in London's Berkeley Square and the Canadian Forces Head-
quarters in Ottawa), raised an issue of continuity of another sort. The
disappearance of patrimonial property in the shape of Frigolet-period
records and archives symptomized the sense of discontinuity that was

56 'Protocol of Canonical Visitation of the Priory "Our Lady of England", Storrington, 22–5 June 1981.' Tongerlo Archives, E2 Engeland en Storrington, Box 7, 58.

57 'Canonry of Our Lady of England, Storrington. Minutes of the Canonry
Chapter held at Storrington, 20–2 April, 1982. Tongerlo Archives, E2 Engeland en
Storrington, Box 7, 58.

a natural consequence of the rupture with the French (or Provençal) past.[58] No one—except some members of the laity—knew who they were, those canons and lay-brothers buried beyond the cloister wall. Today, as the present writer noted on a visit on 22 June 2023, whereas the row of post-War burial sites of Tongerlo canons is marked with sturdy memorials carrying full details of the occupants in the graves below, only a set of rough crosses, already much deteriorated and the inscribed names illegible, exists to show where the remains of the—considerably more numerous—canons and lay-brothers of Frigolet lie awaiting the General Resurrection.

But a metamorphosis of quite another kind was in the offing. Andrew Smith (1944–2021), born at Middlesbrough and entering the Norbertine novitiate in 1963, ordained in 1970 (perhaps tellingly, in the eponymous diocese) and serving first at Crowle and then at Manchester, became in turn sub-prior and novice-master of Storrington, and then in 1992, by way of succession to Prior Gallagher, the superior of the house, and parish priest to boot. At Storrington this union of two roles (prior and *parochus*), familiar in the English houses of Tongerlo canons, had not been usual—not, at any rate, since 1912, which was rather a long time ago. His arrival as head of the canonry heralded a sea-change in what the characteristic discourse of post-Conciliar Catholicism would term its 'style'.

Prior Smith's ideas of liturgy, the environmental space which houses it, and the decorative accoutrements thereof, placed him rather firmly on the Progressive side of the post-Conciliar divide. For those able to decode such announcements, the information provided by *The Arundel and Brighton News* was telling. 'Our parish priest, Father Andrew, normally welcomes his congregation at Mass on Sunday to what he often describes as a gathering of God's family, a Community of Love.'[59] A younger confrère, Paul MacMahon (born 1955), collaborated with him on matters liturgical. MacMahon commissioned music from the American Lutheran composer Marty Haugen (born 1950), later a member of the 'Uniting Church of Christ', a body combining Congregationalist,

---

58 There is some reason to think many papers held at Storrington were lost there during World War II. Correspondence exchanged between Ian Gilbert McLean (1939–2020) of Storrington and senior military officials in England and Canada in the course of 1968, and held in the Muston Archives, is based on that presupposition. A large number of letters from pious correspondents of Storrington survive from the years immediately before, during, and after the First World War, but the supply mysteriously dries up in 1922. Frigolet Archives, Cartons Storrington, E32 and E33. Perhaps significantly, 1922 was the year when the canons finally left Leffe and returned to Frigolet, a desirable but disruptive move.

59 *Arundel and Brighton News*, July 1996.

Calvinist and Lutheran elements). Some would describe it, perhaps unfairly, as adhering to the 'happy clappy' school. The classic arrangement of the conventual church, with two sets of choir stalls so placed as to facilitate antiphonal singing of psalmody, and articulating the space between altar and nave, was imaginatively if uncompromisingly revised. With the help of Italian carpenters, the canons' stalls were re-sited in a semi-circle where once the altar had stood. A new altar now served as focus for the space between canons and people, while the sacrament house, the Eucharistic tabernacle, was moved into a separate chapel on the east side of the building. In a pattern replicated in many places in the Western Catholicism of those years, these changes did not gladden all hearts.

Andrew Smith was not without ambitions for the mission as a whole. The diocesan newspaper could describe in 1997 how two of the Fathers, George Joye and Paul MacMahon, had been sent to initiate a Premonstratensian presence in the church of St Mary Magdalen, Brighton.[60] Oddly enough, the Frigolet canons had considered this in 1904, but the discussion with the vicar general of Southwark had proved abortive. The Brighton experiment was short-lived. The withdrawal of the canons, whose numbers had reached four, was flagged up three years later in the summer of 2000.[61] Like Cincinnatus (*c.* 519 to *c.* 430 BC), the Storrington envoys at 'London by the Sea' returned to their country pursuits.

An attempt was made to capitalize on those thirty-five acres acquired by Prior Colwell. Back at Storrington, trees were planted in the adjoining fields ('Matt's Wood') to provide a quiet Retreat for the public and the outdoor statue of Our Lady of England re-located to that venue.[62] A small vineyard was created, climate change having advanced that far. In 2009, so the online *Great British Vineyards Guide* reported, the first major harvest, consisting of grapes of the pinot noir and chardonnay varieties, yielded some 4000 kilos of fruit, sufficient to make 1,300 bottles of wine. It might have been considered a symbolic re-integration of Tongerlo (Flemish efficiency) and Frigolet (vini-culture and wonderful climate). But as my Conclusion will record, things did not turn out quite like that.

60 *Ibid.*, September 1997,
61 *Ibid.*, June 2000.
62 Here I must thank Mr Philip Orpwood for his kindness in showing me round the remaining territorial properties of the canonry of Muston at Storrington during my visit to the latter on 22 June 2023.

∽ 10 ∽

Conclusion

BY 1987 the presence of the Premonstratensians in Lincolnshire's North Holland, and its overflow in neighbouring South Yorkshire, had come to an end. By 2008 the same was true of South Holland as well. The two Lincolnshire priories of Crowle and Spalding, despite the presence of lay-brothers unnoticed by successive numbers of the *Catholic Directory*, had never enjoyed a sufficiently numerous membership to guarantee a form of conventual life that could replicate the Abbey life of Tongerlo. But as could be seen from the internal disposition of their churches, they were at least intended to be miniatures of the Abbey in their manner of life. The other Norbertine parishes in these areas were, in an analogous kind of way, comparable, therefore, to the 'incorporated' parishes of an Abbey. Since the Lincolnshire priories were never independent canonries the term could hardly be invoked in its strict significance. The only juridical incorporation they could enjoy would be with Tongerlo, or, after the erection of Storrington as an independent canonry in 1962, with the newly promoted Sussex foundation.

The one priory—and indeed the one parish—from the Tongerlo patrimony which seemed assured of survival was Manchester. That was for a straightforward reason. In 2004, in consequence of internal disagreements among the English canons ('English' by residence, since there were occasional Scots and Irishmen as well as Belgians among them), Corpus Christi had been erected as an independent canonry to complement, if not rival, the existing canonry of Storrington, itself, of course, originated not from Tongerlo but Frigolet. (Frigolet canons had laboured, but Tongerlo canons had reaped the reward.) But as Chapter 4 ('Dark Satanic Mills: From Tongerlo to Manchester') has described, the physical state of the basilica—a building which, before the invention of high-rise apartment blocks, must have dwarfed its immediate neighbourhood—proved a burden economically impossible to sustain. By contrast, Storrington, thanks to the Fitzalan-Howard dukes of Norfolk and the acquisitions policy of Prior Colwell, was asset-rich but chronically short of ready money. In due course, as some of the value of its

107

assets was realized by sale, its canonry would become wealthy. But by then it was not money but men who were lacking.

These considerations of money and manpower explain the current configuration of the Order in England. The Manchester canons found for a shortish while a solution (2006–8) within the great Northern city: St Chad's at Cheetham Hill, the mother church of Mancunian Catholicism,[1] which had been loaned them for this purpose by the tenth bishop of Salford, Terence Brain (born 1938).[2] In 2008 the Manchester canonry transferred lock, stock and proverbial barrel to Chelmsford, the county town of Essex, at the invitation of Thomas McMahon (born 1936), the sixth bishop of Brentwood. Its tripartite site (a former Servite convent and two parish churches), was not readily compatible with the development of a fully observant Norbertine life. To the loss of the Catholic Church in Essex where, under the leadership of the prior of Chelmsford, Hugh Allan (born 1967), they were blessed by a trio of highly capable and still youthful priestly vocations, but in accord, nevertheless, with an impulse deriving directly from the Premonstratensian charism, they moved again in 2022 to Peckham, in south-east London. There John Wilson (born 1968), the fifth archbishop of Southwark, was able to offer them a church with a substantial house, monastic in feel, and with outbuildings, notably an enormous hall, which, finance allowing, could serve both parish and the wider south-east London population.

For the successors to Tongerlo's Corpus Christi priory have responsibility for a densely populated parish, with a majority Black population, chiefly West African (Nigeria, Ghana, Sierra Leone), with some elements from the Caribbean, as well as Filipino and other minorities. They worship in a typical Neo-Gothic building of the English Catholic Revival, the work of the younger Pugin, Edward Welby (1834–75), and conveniently provided by its Capuchin Franciscan founders with a generously proportioned chancel suited to the choral celebration of the Liturgy of the Hours. With lively preaching to congregations of a size

---

1 Opened at its original site in Rook Street in 1776: Peter Francis Lupton, *Roland Broomhead, Apostle of the North, 1751–1820* (Leominster: Gracewing, 2015), p. 64.

2 Thus Stephen Cansse, O.Praem. (1929–2008), by dying on holiday in Belgium in September 2008, could be described in the Muston Necrology as 'of Corpus Christ canonry in St Chad's, Manchester'. Cansse, by the way, was plainly a 'trooper', and his career in many ways sums up the story of 'Modern Norbertines in Britain'. Born in Ghent, after his ordination at Tongerlo in 1956 he was sent to St Norbert's College, Storrington, to teach; at independence he became sub-prior and novice-master; he was the last Norbertine parish priest of Crowle (1977–83), and then the last at Stainforth (1983). In 1990 he became parish priest of Storrington but retired owing to ill-health and at the time of the division of the English canonry into two became a founder member of the newly independent canonry at Miles Platting.

and age-range that parish priests in much of contemporary England could only dream of, their liturgy is solemn in its ethos: the weekday conventual Mass is celebrated *ad orientem*, and the music tradition they are establishing includes not only an inherited vernacular hymnody but also plainsong and polyphony. There are few places in London, or indeed in Britain, where people have the opportunity to participate in a Holy Week Triduum featuring a polyphonic Tenebrae.

At Peckham, the earlier modern tradition of titular abbots has been revived in a serendipitous way, through the nomination in 2016 of the prior, Father Hugh Allan, as Administrator Apostolic of the Falkland Islands (with concurrent responsibility, on the other side of the South Atlantic, for Ascension Island, Tristan da Cunha and St Helena). That prompted the Premonstratensian abbot-general, on a nod from the Holy See, to revive the defunct honour of abbot of Beeleigh (in Essex — a reflection of the Chelmsford phase in the story of this rather peripatetic group).[3] Like the leasing (not sale) of Storrington, that gesture toward the glories of the English Premonstratensian past could be regarded as the flying of a flag which might one day signal a different future.

At Storrington, matters did not proceed so smoothly. A reduced community struggled on till 2012, having it in mind toward the close of that period to vacate the priory for a purpose-built dwelling-house close at hand. It was more suited to a quartet of canons than was a monastery built for thirty. But when Andrew Smith, who alone among them had experience as a former Religious superior, became acting parish priest of Filey, in the East Riding of Yorkshire, it seemed simpler, all things considered, to transfer the canonry itself to a nearby village, Muston, where an Anglican rectory in the erstwhile grand manner was on the market.

In 2013 the surviving members of the Storrington canonry leased, therefore, priory, church, and hall to Chemin Neuf, a 'new [Catholic] movement' founded in 1973 in Lyon by a French Jesuit, Laurent Fabre (born 1940), on the understanding that Chemin Neuf would itself sub-let the church to the diocese of Arundel and Brighton, which, through their good offices, also has access to the parish hall and other space.[4] Chemin Neuf seems to have specialized in taking over the declining Religious houses of Catholic England, acquiring the priory of the Olivetan Benedictines at Cockfosters in North London and Sclerder abbey near Polperro in Cornwall, for most of its history a Carmelite nunnery. It is at any rate French, in that way paralleling the origins of Norbertine Storrington.

3 For the mediaeval abbey, see Colvin, *The White Canons in England*, pp. 101–3.
4 Information provided by the Muston agent at Storrington, Mr Philip Orpwood, in an e-mail of 15 June 2023.

And one could say that, as a community of a combined charismatic and ecumenical character it is as typical of the later-twentieth-century French Church as the aspirations of Edmond Boulbon, with his attempted synthesis of Cîteaux and Cluny, were typical of the Catholic France of the mid-nineteenth century. Still, the lease arrangement, rather than change of ownership, between Chemin Neuf and the survivors of Storrington Priory, expressed a hope of revival in some distant, though not perhaps impossibly remote, future.[5]

Meanwhile its successor house, the former Anglican rectory on the Yorkshire Wolds National Trail, now St Mary's Priory, Muston, while reduced (only two canons are left), provides at least a base for pastoral assistance in the parishes of the north Yorkshire coast, from Bridlington to Scarborough. It also has some hopes of securing its future by other means. The *Communicator*, an online bulletin of the English-speaking Circary of the Order of Prémontré, announced that negotiations had begun between the duo of canons at Muston and the historic abbey of Strahov, in Prague, where the sainted founder of the Norbertines lies buried.[6] The attraction of the tiny English canonry to the Czechs lies in the magnetic draw of the Centre for Catholic Studies at the University of Durham, and the desirability of young canons in the Czech lands learning English, perhaps in the nearby language schools of decayed but still populous Scarborough. The Administrator of Muston, Father Thomas Swaffer (born 1966), to whom is owed the beauty of the parsonage house and garden, has conceived this imaginative scheme for English-Bohemian co-operation as one way in which the 'Return of the White Canons' might be sustained.

There we must leave their story, with both achievements and disappointments, high points and low. Only the history that has God as its author will tell how the 'Return' will work out in the generations to come. But certainly possibilities of more than one kind are to hand.

---

5 I am grateful to Father Saba Al Andary and Mrs Samar Al Andary, and the Revd Charles Hadley and Mrs Felicity Hadley, members of the ecumenical organization Chemin Neuf, who currently lease the priory, for showing me round so graciously on my visit of 22 June 2023—and to Mr Philip Orpwood, the agent of the Muston Canonry who own the property, for pointing out salient features of the surroundings which figure in the history of the priory, either in its Frigolet or in its Tongerlo incarnations.

6 Thomas Swaffer, O.Praem., 'Muston Chronicle', *Communicator* 39/1 (2023), p. 36. This magnificent abbey profited by the decision of president Václav Havel in 1990 to recognize without further ado the legal existence of Religious communities. Unlike the other Norbertine abbeys of Bohemia and Moravia, its fabric had been exceptionally well maintained under Communism by the happy accident of use as the National Museum of Czech Literature: Dauzet, *L'Ordre de Prémontré*, p. 542.

BIBLIOGRAPHY

Abercrombie, Nigel, *The Life and Work of Edmund Bishop* (London: Longmans, 1959)

Allchin, A. M., *The Silent Rebellion. Anglican Religious Communities, 1845–1900* (London: SCM Press, 1958)

Anonymous, *The Catholic Directory for the Clergy and Laity of Scotland, 1880* (Edinburgh: Chisholm, 1880)

—— *The Catholic Directory for the Clergy and Laity of Scotland, 1882* (Edinburgh: Chisholm, 1882)

—— *The Catholic Directory for the Clergy and Laity of Scotland, 1890* (Edinburgh: Aberdeen University Press, 1890)

—— *The Catholic Directory for the Clergy and Laity of Scotland, 1893* (Aberdeen: A. King & Co., 1893)

—— *Catholic Directory for the Clergy and Laity of Scotland, 1958* (Glasgow: John S. Burns and Sons, 1958)

   Catholic Directory, Ecclesiastical Register and Almanac for the Year of Our Lord 1872 (London: Burns, Oates, & Co., 1872)

—— *The Catholic Directory, Ecclesiastical Register and Almanac for the Year of Our Lord 1875* (London: Burns, Oates, & Co., 1875)

—— *The Catholic Directory, Ecclesiastical Register and Almanac for the Year of Our Lord 1897* (London: Burns, Oates, & Co., 1897)

—— *Catholic Directory for Scotland, 1999* (Glasgow: John S. Burns and Sons, 1999)

—— *Corpus Christi, Miles Platting, 1889–1989. The First 100 Years* (n. p.; no publisher, 1989)

—— 'Historical Sketch of the Catholic Church at Ambleside', *The Parishioner* XIV. 9 (1934), pp. 21–3

—— *Our Lady of the Sacred Heart, Weston-in-Arden. A Parish History 1849–2004* (Bulkington: no publisher, 2004)

—— *Records of the English Province of the Society of Jesus. Historic Facts illustrative of the Labours and Sufferings of its Members in the Sixteenth and Seventeenth Centuries*, [Volume II = 'Second, Third, and Fourth Series'] (London: Manresa Press, 1875)

—— *St Norbert's Parish, Crowle. Centenary Booklet, 1872–1972* (Storrington: Norbertine Press, 1972)

—— 'The Young Family', re-printed from *Records of the English Province of the Society of Jesus* (n. p., n. d.)

Archbold, W. A. J., 'Makkarell or Mackarell, Matthew' in *Dictionary of National*

Return of the White Canons

Biography (London: Smith, Elder, and Co., 1885–1900), Volume 35, sub loc.

Ardura, Bernard [O.Praem.], *L'abbaye Saint-Michel de Frigolet, 1858–2008. Un siècle et demi d'histoire des Prémontrés en Provence* (Paris, Les-Plans-sur-Bex: Parole et Silence, 2008)

—— *Au Coeur de la Provence. L'Abbaye Saint-Michel de Frigolet* (Rome: no publisher, 2000).

—— 'Biographie du Père Edmond Boulbon', in his (ed.) *Création et tradition à Saint-Michel de Frigolet* (Frigolet: Abbaye Saint-Michel, 1984), pp. 9–20

—— *Prémontrés. Histoire et spiritualité* (Saint-Etienne: Université de Saint-Etienne, 1995)

—— *Premostratensi. Novi secoli di storia e spiritualitàdi un grande Ordine Religioso* (Bologna: Edizioni Studio Domenicano, 1997)

—— 'Les tentatives de restauration de l'Ordre de Prémontré en France au XIXe siècle', in Guy Bedouelle (ed.), *Lacordaire. Son pays, ses amis et la liberté des ordres religieux en France* (Paris: Cerf, 1991), pp. 265–89

—— (ed.), *Création et tradition à Saint-Michel de Frigolet* (Frigolet: Abbaye Saint-Michel, 1984)

Backmund, Norbert, *Monasticon Praemonstratense* (Straubing: Attenkofersche Buchdruckerei, 1949–56, 3 volumes, revised edition Berlin–New York, Walter de Gruyter, 1983)

Badeni, June, *The Slender Tree. A Life of Alice Meynell* (Padstow: Tabb House, 1981)

Bate, Jonathan, *Soul of the Age: The Life, Mind and World of William Shakespeare* (London: Viking, 2008)

Beck, George Andrew, A. A. (ed.), *The English Catholics 1850–1950. Essays to commemorate the centenary of the restoration of the hierarchy of England and Wales* (London: Burns and Oates, 1950)

Boardman, Brigid M., *Between Heaven and Charing Cross. The Life of Francis Thompson* (New Haven, CT: Yale University Press, 1988)

—— (ed.), *The Poems of Francis Thompson. A New Edition* (London and New York: Continuum, 2001)

Bourdarias, Jean, *Père Werenfried, un géant de la charité* (Paris: Fayard, 1996)

Bowker, Margaret, 'Mackarell (Makkarell), Matthew', *Oxford Dictionary of National Biography*, Volume 35, (New York: Oxford University Press, 2004), pp. 494–5

Brangwyn, Frank, *The Way of the Cross. An Interpretation,*with a Commentary by G. K. Chesterton (London: Hodder and Stoughton, 1935)

Brangwyn, Rodney, *Brangwyn* (London: William Kimber, 1978)

Bullivant, Stephen, *Mass Exodus: Catholic Disaffiliation in Britain and America since Vatican II* (Oxford: Oxford University Press, 2019, 2nd edition)

Cassidy, Peter, 'La fondation du Prieuré Notre-Dame d'Angleterre à Storrington', in Bernard Ardura (ed.), *Création et Tradition à Saint-Michel de Frigolet* (Frigolet: Abbaye Saint-Michel, 1984), pp. 95–8

Celen, V., *Priester-Schilder Esser* (Turnhout: no publisher, n. d.)

Champ, Judith F., *William Bernard Ullathorne, 1806–1889. A Different Kind of Monk* (Leominster: Gracewing, 2006)

Bibliography

—— (ed.), *Oscott College, 1838–1988. A Volume of Commemorative Essays* (Sutton Coldfield: Oscott College, 1988)

Clercq, Donatien de, O.Praem., 'Monseigneur Thomas Louis Heylen', in Dominique-Marie Dauzet, Martine Plouvier, Cécile Souchon (ed.), *Les Prémontrés au XIXe siècle: traditions et renouveau* (Paris: Cerf, 2000), pp. 261–9

Colvin, H. M., *The White Canons in England* (Oxford: Clarendon Press, 1951)

Cook, M. G., *Edward Prior: Arts and Crafts Architect* (Marlborough: Crowood Press, 2015)

Cowan, Ian B., and David E. Easson, *Medieval Religious Houses: Scotland, with an Appendix on the Houses in the Isle of Man* (London and New York: Longmans, 1976, 2nd edition)

Crews, Clyde F., *English Catholic Modernism. Maude Petre's Way of Faith* (Notre Dame, IN: University of Notre Dame Press, 1984).

Cuyper, Ronny de, *Joannes Chrysostomus de Swert, vijftigste abt van Tongerlo, 1867/8–1887* (Leuven: Katholieke Universiteit, 1981)

Dale, Alzina Stone, *The Art of G. K. Chesterton* (Chicago, IL: Loyola University Press, 1985)

Danner, Franciscus (ed.), *Catalogus totius Sacri, Candidi, Canonici ac Exempti Ordinis Praemonstratensis ineunte anno 1894*, (Innsbruck: Felicianus Rauch, 1894)

Dauzet, Dominique-Marie, 'Jean Chrysostome de Swert, abbé de Tongerlo (1834–1887) à travers sa correspondance', in Martine Plouvier (ed.), *Abbatiat et abbés dans l'Ordre de Prémontré* (Turnhout: Brepols, 2015), pp. 377–90

—— *L'Ordre de Prémontré. Neuf cents ans d'histoire* (Paris: Salvator, 2021)

—— *Petite vie de saint Norbert* (Paris: Desclée de Brouwer, 2013)

Durand, J.-P., *La Liberté des congrégations religieuses en France. Régimes français des congrégations religieuses* (Paris: Cerf, 1999)

Durix, Claude, *Norbert Calmels. Histoire d'une amitié, 1944–1985* (Paris: Guy Trédaniel, 1986)

Dyck, Leo C. van, 'Les chapitres généraux de l'Ordre au XIXe siècle: renaissance d'une institution', in Dominique-Marie Dauzet, Martine Plouvier, Cécile Souchon (ed.), *Les Prémontrés au XIXe siècle: traditions et renouveau* (Paris: Cerf, 2000), pp. 175–92

—— 'Evermodus P. H. Backx, de tweede stichter van de abdij van Tongerlo. Bidrage tot een levenscheets, 1835–1845', *De Lindeboom* [Tilburg], V (1981), pp. 158–204

—— *The Norbertine Abbey of Tongerlo* (Westerlo-Tongerlo: Norbertijnenabdij & Stichting Monumenten en Landscapszorg, n. d.)

Engels, Friedrich, *The Condition of the Working Class in England*, edited by David McLellan (Oxford: Oxford University Press, 2009 [1845]),

Everson, Paul, and David Stocker, *Custodians of Continuity? The Premonstratensian Abbey at Barlings and the Landscape of Ritual* (Sleaford: Heritage Trust of Lincolnshire, 2011)

Finn, Richard, *The Dominicans in the British Isles and Beyond: a new history of the English Province of the Friars Preachers* (Cambridge: Cambridge University Press, 2022)

Fletcher, T. W., 'The Great Depression of English Agriculture, 1873–1896' in P. J. Perry (ed.), *British Agriculture, 1875–1914* (London: Methuen, 1973)

Fordham, Edward T., *A History of the Catholic Church of the Immaculate Conception and St Norbert* (Spalding: n. publisher, 1992)

Fourvière, Xavier de [Albert Rieux], *Escourregudo en Anglo-Terro (Promenade en Angleterre). L'Angleterre du XIXe siècle vue par un Provençal* (Marseille: Editions Jeanne Laffitte, 2005)

Francis, Ian, Stuart Holmes and Bruce Yardley, *The Lake District. Landscape and Geology* ((Crowwood Presss, Ramsbury, Marlborough, 2022)

Geraghty, Anthony, *The Empress Eugénie in England. Art, Architecture, Collecting* (Chicago, IL: University of Chicago Press, 2022)

Gidney, Alan, *The Parish and Church of St Norbert's, Crowle. 125 Years of Catholicism in Crowle* (Crowle: no publisher, 1999)

Gillett, H. M., *[The] Shrine of Our Lady of England at Storrington* (Exeter: Catholic Records Press, 1954)

—— 'Storrington: Our Lady of England', in his *Shrines of Our Lady in England and Wales* (London: Samuel Walker, 1957)

Gooch, Leo, 'Henry O'Callaghan: Manning's Reluctant Episcopal Protégé', in Sheridan Gilley (ed.), *Victorian Churches and Churchmen. Essays presented to Vincent Alan McClelland* (Woodbridge: Boydell Press, 2005), pp. 58–74

Goovaerts, André Léon, *Ecrivains, artistes et savants de l'Ordre de Prémontré. Dictionnaire bio-bibliographique* (Brussels: Société belge de librairie, 1899–1916, 4 volumes)

Greensted, Mary, *The Arts and Crafts Movement in Britain* (Oxford: Shire, 2010)

Gribbin, Joseph A., *The Premonstratensian Order in Late Mediaeval England* (Woodbridge: Boydell and Brewer, 2012)

Guilday, Peter, *The English Catholic Refugees on the Continent, I. The English Colleges and Convents in the Catholic Low Countries, 1558–1795* (London: Longmans, 1914)

Ham, Joan, *Victorian and Edwardian Storrington* (Chichester: Phillimore, 1983)

Hannah, Rosemary, *The Grand Designer: Third Marquess of Bute* (Edinburgh: Birlinn, 2012)

Higham, Placid, O. S. B., 'The Early Annals of St Michael's Farnborough', *Pax* XLIX. 290 (Summer, 1959), pp. 44–50,

—— *St Michael's Benedictine Abbey. A History and Guide* (Farnborough: Community of St Michael's Abbey, n. d.)

Hoyle, R. W., *The Pilgrimage of Grace and the Politics of the 1530s* (Oxford: Oxford University Press, 2001)

Hunter-Blair, Oswald, *John Patrick, Third Marquess of Bute, K. T., (1847–1900). A Memoir* (London: Murray, 1921)

—— 'Whithorn Priory', *Catholic Encyclopaedia* (New York: Robert Appleton, 1907–12), vol. 15, *s.v.*

Jansen, J. E., *Monseigneur Thomas-Louis Heylen, évêque de Namur. Son action sociale et religieuse pendant vingt-cinq ans d'épiscopat* (Namur: Wesmael-Charlier, 1924)

John, Catherine Rachel, 'Donald Attwater, 1892–1977: A Man for His Time and Ours', *Chesterton Review* 29. 4 (2003), pp. 519–27

Kelly, James T. (ed.), *The Letters of Baron Friedrich von Hügel and Maude D. Petre* (Leuven: Peeters, 2003)

Koch, John T. (ed.), 'Ninian, St.', *Celtic Culture. A Historical Encyclopedia* (Santa Barbara, CA: ABC-Clio, 2006), Volume IV, p. 1358

Kollar, René, 'Religious Orders', in Sally Mitchell (ed.), *Victorian Britain. An Encyclopedia* (New York, and London: Garland, 1988), pp. 666–7

Korthals-Alles, J., *Sir Cornelius Vermuyden: The Lifework of a great Anglo-Dutchman in Land Reclamation and Drainage* (London: Williams and Norgate, 1925)

Lamy, Hugues, 'L'oeuvre des Bollandistes à l'abbaye de Tongerlo', *Analecta Praemonstratensia* II (1926), pp. 294–306, 379–89; III (1927), pp. 61–79, 156–78, 284–313

Leveritt, Norman, and Michael J. Elsden, *Aspects of Spalding, 1790–1930* (Spalding: Chameleon, 1986)

Lokando, Richard Dane, *Prémontrés et dominicains belges au Congo: Uele 1898–1924* (Paris: L'Harmattan, 2018)

Loth, Arthur, *Sister Rose: Her Life and Work and The Mass of Reparation*, translated by Martin Roestenburg, O.Praem. (Waterloo, ON: Arouca Press, 2021)

Lupton, Peter Francis, *Roland Broomhead, Apostle of the North, 1751–1820* (Leominster: Gracewing, 2015)

McClean, Ian, O.Praem., 'Le Prieuré de Notre Dame d'Angleterre', in Dominique-Marie Daudet, Martine Plouvier, Cécile Souchon (ed.), *Les Prémontrés au XIXe siècle: Traditions et renouveaux* (Paris: Cerf, 2000), pp. 239–43.

McGrath, Francis, J. F. M. S. (ed.), *Letters and Diaries of John Henry Newman*, XXXII, Supplement (Oxford: Oxford University Press, 2008), pp. 471–2

Macdougall, Norman, *An Antidote to the English: The Auld Alliance, 1295–1560* (East Linton: Tuckwell Press, 2001)

McInally, Mary, *Edward Ilsley, Bishop of Birmingham 1888–1911, Archbishop of Birmingham 1911–1921* (London: Burns Oates, 2002)

MacRaild, Donald M., *Culture, Conflict and Migration. The Irish in Victorian Cumbria* (Liverpool: Liverpool University Press, 1998)

—— *Irish Migrants in Modern Britain, 1750–1922* (Basingstoke: Macmillan, 1999)

Marshall, Brian, *Cockersand Abbey. A Lancashire House of Premonstratensian Canons, 1180–1539* (Staining: Landy Publishing, 2001)

Mole, Simon, *Catholic Life in Storrington. The Comings and Goings since 1880* (n.p.: no publisher, 2022)

Monks of St Michael's Abbey, *St Michael's Abbey, Farnborough* (Andover: Pitkin Unichrome, 1998)

Monnier, H., *Le Rèverendissime Père Léon Perrier, abbé de Saint-Michel de Frigolet, 1881–1948* (Frigolet: Abbaye Saint-Michel, 1948)

Moore, Chris, *Betrayal of Trust. The Father Brendan Smyth Affair and the Catholic Church* (Dublin: Marino, 1995)

Mostyn, Dorothy A., *The Story of a House. The History of Farnborough Hill* (Farnborough: St Michael's Abbey Press, 1999 [1980])

Nichols, Aidan, O. P., *Artist and Monk. Dom Theodore Baily (1898–1966), Iconography and the Renewal of the Liturgical Arts in England* (Leominster: Gracewing, 2014)

Norman, Edward, *The English Catholic Church in the Nineteenth Century* (Oxford: Clarendon Press, 1984)

—— *Roman Catholicism in England from the Elizabethan Settlement to the Second Vatican Council* (New York: Oxford University Press, 1985)

O'Neil, Robert, M. H. M., *Cardinal Herbert Vaughan, Archbishop of Westminster, Bishop of Salford, Founder of the Mill Hill Missionaries* (Tunbridge Wells: Burns & Oates, 1975)

Parker, Joanna and Corinna Wagner (ed.), *The Oxford Handbook of Victorian Medievalism* (Oxford; Oxford University Press, 2020)

Paxton, Nicholas, 'The Imperial Abbey at Farnborough, 1883–1920', *Recusant History* 28. 4 (2007), pp. 575–92

Petre, Maude, *Autobiography and Life of George Tyrrell* (London: Edward Arnold, 1912), 2 volumes

Phillips, Peter. *John Lingard, Priest and Historian* (Leominster: Gracewing, 2008)

Ravary, Berthe, *Prémontré dans la tourmente révolutionnaire. La vie de Jean-Baptiste L'Ecuy, dernier abbé général des Prémontrés en France, 1740–1834* (Paris: Grasset, 1955)

Reuss, Basil R., 'A Norbertine Pope?', *Catholic Historical Review* 19. 2 (1933), pp. 200–2

Ritchie, Anna, 'From Colonsay to Whithorn: the work of a 19th century antiquary, William Galloway'. *Proceedings of the Society of Antiquaries of Scotland* 142 (2013), pp. 435–356

Robinson, John Martin, *The Dukes of Norfolk* (Chichester: Phillimore, 1995, 2nd edition)

Sagovsky, Nicholas, *On God's Side. A Life of George Tyrrell* (Oxford: Clarendon Press, 1990)

Schofield, Nicholas, and Gerard Skinner, *The English Cardinals* (Oxford: Family Publications, 2007)

Serrou, R., and P. Vals, *Les Prémontrés. Chez les Pères Blancs de Frigolet, Préface de Marcel Pagnol, de l'Académie française* (Paris: Pierre Horay, 1958)

Seward, Desmond, *Eugénie. The Empress and her Empire* (Stroud: Sutton, 2004)

Shenton, Kenneth, *O My Hornby and My Barlow Long Ago. The Life of the Poet Francis Thompson, 1859–1907* (Nantwich: Max Books, 2019)

Smith, W. H. C., *The Empress Eugénie and Farnborough* (Winchester: Hampshire County Council, 2001)

—— 'Les Prémontrés et l'impératrice Eugénie á Farnborough en 1887', In Dominique-Marie Dauzet, Martine Plouvier, Cécile Souchon (ed.), *Les Prémontrés au XIXe siècle: traditions et renouveau* (Paris: Cerf, 2000), pp. 230–7

Smith, William Matthew, C. R. P., *St Joseph and St Nicholas, Moorends. Golden Jubilee, 1939–1989* (n. p., n. publisher, 1989)

Sollier, J. F., 'Frédéric-François-Xavier Ghislain de Mérode', in *Catholic Encyclopaedia* (New York: Robert Appleton, 1907–12), sub loc.

Spilbeeck, Waltman van, *De abdij van Tongerloo. Geschiedkundige navorsingen* (Lier and Geel: Taymans-Nezy, 1888, reprinted in facsimile Averbode: Abdij Averbode, 1997)

Thompson, A. Hamilton, *The Premonstratensian Abbey of Welbeck* (London: Faber and Faber, 1938)

Tour d'Allaine, Jean de la, *Le siège de Frigolet. Poème épique en trois chants* (Aix: Nicot, 1880)

Turquand, E. D., 'The Lincolnshire Bulb Industry', *Scientific Horticulture* 23 (1971), pp. 67–74

Vedel, Romain, *Un homme de Dieu, le Réverendissime Päère Adrien Borelly, abbé de Saint-Michel de Frigolet, 1838–1931* (Avignon: Aubanel, 1932)

Vita metrica sancti patris Norberti auctore Fratre Joanne Chrysostomo, abbate Tongerloënsi, O.Praem. (Namur: 1886)

Wall, Arthur G., *Some Bedworth Catholic History* (Birmingham: The Shakespeare Press, n. d.)

Walsh, John Evangelist (ed.), *The Letters of Francis Thompson* (New York: Hawthorn Books, 1969)

Wilcox, Timothy (ed.), *Eric Gill and the Guild of St Joseph and St Dominic* (Hove: Hove Museum and Art Gallery, 1990)

Wilson, A. N., *Hilaire Belloc. A Biography* (London: Hamish Hamilton, 1984)

INDEX OF NAMES

INDEX OF PLACES

www.ingramcontent.com/pod-product-compliance
Lightning Source LLC
Chambersburg PA
CBHW022026090426
42739CB00006BA/312